4/2/82

Along Our Country Road

by Otha D. Wearin

Illustrated by Felix Summers

Published in United States of America by
WALLACE-HOMESTEAD BOOK COMPANY
BOX BI
DES MOINES, IOWA 50304

Dedicated to
all the men, women and children
who have ever
lived and worked on a farm

Printed in the U.S.A.

INTRODUCTION

When we realize that farming is the oldest business on the face of the earth, it is easier to comprehend how such a tremendous variety of legends and folk practices have surrounded both the industry and the people who have and still are operating it. Archaeologists tell us they have found evidence that human beings were tilling the soil, after a fashion, as much as ten thousand years ago. No wonder farmers are a stubborn lot. The basic principles of planting seed, cultivating young plants, and harvesting the crop have remained the same. The methods and tools have changed. Mechanical progress moved slowly until a half century ago.

In the beginning a human being considered himself fortunate if he could produce enough food to feed himself and his family. Modern methods have equipped him to feed "half a hundred." Such developments have eased his labor but multiplied the problems of his relationship with our economic system. It would be interesting to know just how many thousands of years he has been dodging the sheriff.

It is the older ways that this volume, like its predecessors, endeavors to preserve. These stories don't go back 10,000 years, they recall the ways of farmers around the turn of the century, practices that have disappeared, or at least subsided.

A great American statesman once said, in substance, that "The only light by which our feet are guided is that from the lamp of experience."

If the recollections in this book are entertaining, I will be pleased. If any of them become useful in some emergency of tomorrow, I will be doubly rewarded.

I always feel deeply indebted to a great many people for suggestions, counsel, and assistance in the writing of a book. It is impossible to mention all of them by name.

A few however, my wife Lola, my secretary Lola Hasselquist, Mrs. Glenn Anderson, and Mrs. Jennie Haroff have been especially generous with their time and patience.

Otha D. Wearin
Nishna Vale Farm
Hastings, Iowa 1975

TABLE OF CONTENTS

TABLE OF CONTENTS

8

ALMANACS

The possession of books was a luxury in which few farm families permitted themselves to indulge when the middle-west was growing up. Of course there was a Bible, sometimes a county paper, and most assuredly an almanac. Patent medicine manufacturers issued them to advertise their products. Druggists handed them out to their customers for free.

They were generally about five by eight inches in size, containing some forty to fifty pages, illustrated and usually indexed. In addition to the signs of the Zodiac there were rules of measurement, mathematical tables, and calendars for the past, current, and coming year. Farmers often insisted on regulating their planting, butchering, castrating, and weaning of young stock by the stages of the moon. There were signs for butchering so the meat wouldn't curl when being cooked in the pan.

There was a wealth of other material, both fact and feature, in the almanac. The reader with time to spare on long winter evenings could be enlightened by weather predictions, sometimes remarkably accurate; articles explaining the Northern Lights, America's Blue Laws, How to Read the Palm of Your Hand, Home Games, Postal Information, Correct Dress Chart for Men, What Could be Done With Five Billion Dollars (in case you might have that much someday), How To Identify Rare Coins, and a vast quantity of other valuable and sometimes useless information.

Almanacs issued by manufacturers of various products contained different features in addition to standard information. They were highly prized by farm people and now by collectors. Little wonder when there were no libraries within easy reach of horse and buggy!

The Middle Border would have prevailed without almanacs but not so well. It is still contributing to rural America, with even more information contained in some seventy-five pages, but is seldom considered indispensable. Television and farm editors have replaced the almanac for many professional and amateur farmers and gardeners.

9

RELIGION ON THE BORDER

Preachers were few and far between in the early days of the Middle Border. The scattered settlers had religion but no money to pay a minister's salary. Circuit Riders, yes, but there were long lapses of time between their visits. My grandmother died in October of 1871. There was no one in the area to hold services for her and her family. A traveling minister appeared in the spring and was engaged to preach the funeral sermon. Death under any circumstances was never a pleasant thought, but it was less so in the rural areas than anywhere else. Before the practice of embalming, burial took place within a matter of hours. When the pioneers crossed the plains, many a dear one was laid away in a box in an unmarked grave.

Summer revivals were popular in the rural areas. People would arrive in wagons, buckboards, or on horseback from miles away to attend such meetings, often held in a country schoolhouse or some farmer's grove, occasionally in a tent. The revivalists were the hell and brimstone type who gave you little chance for salvation. Maybe if you stood up and confessed your sins publicly, you might have an outside chance. A local choir helped create the atmosphere of both joy and repentance.

The revivalist usually set up shop for at least a week, having arranged for food and lodging in the household of a country family. My father used to say they were a good thing for the sparsely settled country in at least two ways. Invariably during a week's time, they managed to save a few souls and make a few. Some were made in the nearby woods on summer evenings.

Camp meetings, as they were sometimes called, were a source of renewed religious fervor. They were one of the few sources of entertainment to break the monotony of hard work and loneliness among the pioneers of the Middle Border. The countryside no longer rings to the sound of "Though your sins be as scarlet, they shall be as white as snow," "The Old Rugged Cross," "Onward Christian Soldiers" or "God Be With You 'Till We Meet Again."

NEIGHBORHOOD PICNICS

There was a heart-warming comradeship among neighbors on the Middle Border that guaranteed help in times of trouble, picnics on holidays, and just plain neighborliness. The picnics were something to remember as long as you lived. They were often held in someone's dooryard, now known as a lawn. A flowing stream through someone's land, bordered by pasture land made an ideal spot for a neighborhood gathering on Independence Day.

There was plenty of room to spread out the bountiful food supply on tables improvised with a few one by twelve barnboards on empty barrels or sawhorses. The quality and extent of the food would have made a master chef groan with envy. There were huge platters heaped with golden brown fried chicken, whole baked hams, crocks of potato salad, fruit salad, deviled eggs, sandwiches, an assortment of pies and cakes. There was always a well padded canvas bag containing a five gallon can of vanilla ice cream. Men, women, and children gathered around the food and the ice cream as long as they were still able to swallow.

There were no concessions, no hawkers of cheap merchandise at high prices, no paid performers, and generally not even any fireworks except for a few small fire crackers provided for the children. In all of my youth there was never an injury or a serious accident but there was all kinds of fellowship and good conversation about crops, livestock, householding, exchanging of recipes and even a little politics, especially in election years. The meal over and partially settled, a baseball game, usually "one old cat," got under way.

The ladies gathered to exchange apron patterns, pot holders, discuss new styles and other woman talk. The oldsters among the men spread themselves out on the grass beneath a spreading shade tree. There was no admission charge, no traffic problem, and plenty of free parking for everyone.

14

BARN DANCES

People of the Middle Border were adept at providing their own amusement. They had no choice in the matter if they had a feeling for entertainment, as they often did. Even religious services were infrequent as circuit riders and evangelists appeared only at widely separated intervals. Now and then there was a shucking bee or a quilting party.

The most popular event of all was a barn dance. It was easily and quickly organized. Anybody's barn was suitable if the haymow was empty. A little sweeping, someone to play the fiddle, the drums, maybe a banjo, and the fun started. People came in overalls and calico, sunbonnets and straw hats. Quite frequently the musicians couldn't have read a note of music to save their lives, but the tunes they played had rhythm.

Early barn dances were neighborhood affairs, occurring in the spring and fall when the weather was not too warm or too cold. Turkey in the Straw and Alexander's Ragtime Band were popular numbers. The Virginia Reel or square dances went on until the early morning hours.

Refreshments were simple: apples from cave or orchard, doughnuts, coffee or cider, and pumpkin pie in season. The entertainment was wholesome, and the cost was negligible. Such jolly good times seem to be a forgotten art. In many areas, even the barns are gone. Community buildings and national guard armories in nearby towns have replaced the few barns that still remain as scenes for such revelry. Country people in most areas seem to have allowed the practice of entertaining themselves to become dormant.

PLANK BRIDGES

When a team and buggy traveling at a keen trot crossed an old plank floored bridge across a stream, you could hear the rumbling sound at least a quarter of a mile away. Not only were the floors of wood, but the joists and bannisters were of the same material.

The planks in the floors of the earliest bridges were generally two inches thick by twelve inches wide, but when the thickness was increased to three inches these were known as "bridge plank." In many cases they were not even nailed down. They were held in place by wooden stringers running at right angles to the floor on each side. The planks could not escape on their own as a result of horse drawn vehicles passing over them, even as fast as a horse or team could trot. They did however collide with each other from the motion of vehicles and the pounding of horses hoofs, making a deep-throated rumbling sound. Horses traveling over them and cattle being driven across them often became

frightened. They would crowd together in the center of the bridge, moving more rapidly with every step they took.

It was not unusual for cattle to balk at a wooden bridge and refuse to cross. Extreme caution had to be exercised to keep them from stampeding and retracing their steps. If one of them could be lured onto the bridge, the rest would follow. If cattle to be moved were known to be a little "skittish," a horse drawn load of hay would precede them. Hay was often scattered on the floor of the bridge to tempt them.

We seldom find an old wooden bridge any more unless it is being preserved for historic reasons or is spanning a small stream on a primitive country road. If we had them, they would no longer provide a hazard to the movement of livestock, as it is no longer advisable to drive cattle on country roads in this day of superhighways and stock trucks.

COWHIDE BOOTS

When the border lands were young, men as well as horses and oxen had to be shod for rough work. The metal shoes for the animals could not have been much heavier or more uncomfortable than the cowhide boots that men were forced to wear in the feed yards and for field work.

Some people used to say cowhide boots would wear out your feet before your feet could wear out the boots. In cold weather they would get as stiff as a board. They were not much more pliable in moderately warm weather. The only way you could get them on in the winter time, with any degree of ease, was to park them for the night by the heating stove or the kitchen range. If you didn't you had to put them in the oven to limber them up.

A boot jack, either metal or homemade of wood, or a forked tree limb was required equipment for removing "cowhides" from your feet at night. If they had become wet during the day's work, as they often did, then removal became almost painful. If the bootjack wouldn't pull them you had to sit with your back against the wall while one of the family seized the boot and pulled for dear life.

Walking behind a harrow, a New Departure, a Jenny Lind, or a double shovel cultivator wearing cowhide boots on a hot dusty day was something no one ever forgot. Invariably you came to the house at night with blisters the size of half dollars on your heels. When it came time to cultivate corn, the cowhide boots could usually be found standing at one end of the field or the other. The men, or the "hands" as they were often called, were either barefooted or working in their sock feet. Not many tears have been shed over the passing of walking cultivators or cowhide boots.

LAP-ROBES

What is a lap-robe? Not many people know in this day of air conditioned cars and three hour flights from the Middle Border to either coast.

At the turn of the Twentieth Century no one started anywhere in cold weather without a lap-robe. Not even a top buggy or a carriage afforded much protection against wind and snow. You needed a warm, heavy cover over your knees.

There were a great many varieties of lap-robes. A horse blanket was a favorite cover to protect the occupants on the trip as well as the animal while he had to stand at a hitchrack in below zero weather waiting for the return journey. They were closely woven woolen blankets of considerable weight. Their multicolored stripes blended with anything the occupants of the vehicle might be wearing. Strong leather straps were sewed to the fabric at the proper points for buckling to the harness when the blanket was placed over the horse's body.

In the early days, buffalo robes tanned with the hair on were the pride and joy of many a country family. The passing of the buffalo brought horse hides tanned in the same way into favor. Both types were lined with all-wool cloth, making them warm and flexible. Some affluent farmers invested in blankets made specifically for use as lap-robes, some with waterproofing on one side to shed the rain and snow.

One of Grandmother's quilts was often pressed into use if there was a shortage of lap-robes. All types were useful in the days of horse drawn vehicles. In fact, travel without them would have been difficult with the temperature below zero.

THE PACK PEDDLER

The pack peddler who walked through the country selling his wares had almost disappeared by the time of my advent on the Middle Border. Only a few were still trudging through the country carrying loads of amazing size and weight on their backs. They brought a few luxuries and some necessities from far places to the isolated families of the early west. Their merchandise thrilled the entire family but especially pioneer women who made the greatest sacrifices of all. They had left the finer, delicate things of life behind when they climbed aboard the prairie schooners and headed into unknown country with the men they loved.

How a country wife must have thrilled to see a peddler undo his pack and spread the contents on the cabin floor or even a spot of grass in the door yard if it was nice, windless summer day. Their eyes must have lighted up at the sight of a new bonnet, a tiny silk handkerchief, a cameo breast pin, a tortoise shell comb or even a strand of gold beads for the wife or mother of a more affluent settler. There were pins, needles, thread, embroidery hoops, knitting needles, hand woven linen table cloths, and napkins. Such things were a vision from another world for the country folk, especially the children of the Middle Border who had known such things existed but never dreamed of seeing them right at home.

Purchases had to be for cash. A deal involved considerable haggling and trading. A quantity purchase usually meant a better price, especially if the peddler got his dinner or a night's lodging, which was not uncommon.

The pack peddler not only brought his treasures but bits of news from the outside world and far away neighborhoods. Of course he always hoped to gather as much information as he gave.

Towns began to appear, roads began to improve, the peddler and his pack were soon lost in the dust of the automobile, never again to walk the back country roads of America.

24

A TRAVELING DAIRY

The pioneers and their wagon trains that broke trails across the prairie carried with them only the essentials for life and the defense of it. A milk cow and a bull were two things they never dispensed with except as a last resort to fend off starvation. The milk the cow produced was usually enough to do that except under the most unusual circumstances.

Milk cows were an indispensable part of life on the Middle Border. Milk was important to children and adults. There were no towns within easy reach, no refrigeration in the settlements or on the farm. Fresh milk had to come from the cow night and morning. It kept reasonably well for a few hours or a day and a night if the family had a good cave or a deep well-pit to store it in. There was no question about the importance of cows, they were a necessity for every family. Furthermore, there was butter to be made as well as cottage cheese or smearcase from the whey of skim milk.

Cows of course were milked by hand. Sometimes the housewife assumed the chore at rush season when there was corn to plant or cultivate, or small grain to harvest. No one had ever heard of a milking machine. The nearest thing to it was a firm grip of the hands—and be sure your fingernails were cut short.

The task wasn't too unpleasant when the weather was moderate. It was a different story on a scorching hot summer night, or in the winter when the temperature dropped below zero.

Country people were never out of milk. Now dairy cows are seldom found except where full time dairies are the major source of income. Cream separators, once an important part of every farm unit's milking equipment, have been sold for antiques or adapted to the support of rural mail boxes. Dairy cows that supplied the rural income have gone big business.

BEFORE THE DOCTORS CAME

It was a long time before medical doctors arrived on the Middle Border, much less nurses or hospitals. Early settlers depended upon home remedies that had been handed down from one pioneer household to another. Sometimes it was difficult to determine if they were an effective cure or a witches' brew with a psychological effect.

Every child dreaded to hear the announcement that the time had arrived for the usual spring tonic of sulfur and molasses. The sweetener helped to conceal whatever may have been good about the sulfur. A tablespoon full of the mixture a few nights in a row was enough to fix the memory of spring in your mind for the rest of your life. Sassafras tea made from the bark of the tree bearing the same name was a much more pleasant substitute. A badly sprained ankle called for a good soaking in hot water and epsom salts. If it persisted, a flax seed poultice had to be bound around the foot and left over night to draw out the soreness. Speaking of a poultice, nothing was supposed to be superior to a slick, sleazy, mustard plaster across your chest for a cold that had settled on your lungs. We always hoped the heat it generated would offset the discomfort of tolerating the thing all night.

An open wound called for granny's poultice of moldy bread. It was an early effort to capitalize upon the basic element of penicillin. There is no doubt that it helped to prevent many a serious infection. It was an improvement over a slice of fat meat tied around the injury.

We saved all of the grease from roasting a goose at Thanksgiving or Christmas to apply externally for sinus infection or sore throat. A pleasant relief for the latter was the syrup mother made of brown sugar and vinegar. Of course it had to be preceded by gargling with hot salt water.

Chapped hands from cornshucking or outdoor work called for the gentle relief of mutton tallow. It too was stored in small jars or tin containers and would stay fresh smelling for months at a time. Enterprising mothers and housewives sometimes tempered its aroma with a few drops of rose water or spices.

We doctored sprains on people or animals with a home-made concoction of eggs, turpentine, and vinegar in such proportions that the turpentine wouldn't blister the area that was treated. It was effective. It would not however keep indefinitely without assuming a rather acrid aroma and was then inclined to blister more readily unless applied very sparingly.

Most of the frontier remedies used by pioneers served much the same purpose for domestic animals. However there were specifics such as pine tar for horses with a bad cough. A small blob of it placed on a narrow piece of a wood shingle could be laid on the back of a horse's tongue. It got the same results as an expensive patent remedy.

A cut on a horse often left a hairless scar. An old uncle of mine always got results with sweet oil and iodine. He used to insist that the combination would grow hair on a billiard ball. I can't vouch for the latter but it haired over some unsightly scars on our horses.

An open wound on a quadruped was often treated with a handful of airslacked lime. Once the healing process had been completed, sweet oil and iodine came into play.

Homespun remedies lent a sense of security to the pioneer homes of the Middle Border. A few that have been handed down from generation to generation are still in use. The demise of our country doctor services has given a few home remedies a new lease on life.

HARNESS SHOPS

The harness shop was an important enterprise in every town of any size. A good harness maker was in great demand as were makers of fine saddles. The latter was generally a trade in itself but the two sometimes went together.

A farmer seldom went to town without visiting the harness maker, sometimes to buy a set of harness or a saddle, but more often it was for minor repairs; a hitch rein, collar pads, a more severe bit for an obstreperous horse, an over-check, a breeching strap or a trace chain. Sometimes he carried a pair of saddle stirrups to be leather covered on the front so some "small-fry" could start to ride horseback. Maybe the old saddle needed new cinch straps, or perhaps the tree needed recovering. If he was a real fancy horseman he might buy a Martingale.

The shop itself was a fascinating place for a small boy, in fact for any boy large or small. There was a life size model of a horse, made of plaster of paris with iron legs. The body was covered with cloth and painted, dappled grey, black, bay, or dun color (now known as palomino). The model served to display a set of harness, bridle and all.

A cast iron, wheel type hanger was suspended from the ceiling. Various lengths and colors of rawhide buggy whips from five to eight feet long hung from slots in the wheel. There were sides of tan leather and brown leather in stacks, boxes of buckles of all sizes, snaps and blind buckles. Here and there on the wall or in display cases were glass bull's eye rosettes portraying different colors of horses, horse heads, jaunting cars, dogs, buffalo, etc., fifty cents a pair to decorate the bridles. There were cards of solid metal rosettes with embossed designs of stars, bells, initials, etc.

Every harness shop stocked a good assortment of both factory and hand made saddles. The skirts ranged from plain leather types to highly carved, portraying bucking horses, wild animals, flowers, or geometric designs.

The atmosphere of harness shops was laden with the unique aroma of leather, tempered slightly with that of neatsfoot oil and a touch of wood smoke from the stove at the back of the room. It was a heaven of thrills for lovers of good horses. Just about everyone fell into that category because horses were the sole source of power and transportation.

THE SAGA OF A SETTING HEN

Who among older folk has not been exasperated to wits' end trying to get an old setting hen to stay on her own nest. Most hen houses had an area partitioned off from the rest of the interior for setting. It required three weeks of continuous incubation by the mother hen to hatch a setting of eggs, usually fifteen in number. The "setters" had to have their own quarters to keep layers from adding new eggs until the nest was over-flowing. The original setting would hatch if not crowded out of the nest, but the eggs added had to be farmed out to other "setters" or discarded.

Some hens were ideal mothers, never departing from their task except for a little food and water each day. They were even careful about getting on and off the nest. Now and then a cantankerous old biddie would break some of her eggs, making a foul mess in the nest, requiring what eggs remained to be carefully and gently washed in lukewarm water. The entire contents of straw or hay in the nest had to be replaced with a clean supply. If the hen repeated the process, the project was usually abandoned and the culprit tossed into a slatted crate on a short diet until she surrendered her misguided maternal ambitions.

Hatching chickens with setting hens was a tedious process. The setting hens had to have feed and water at all times. Their special place was dimly lighted and they were disturbed as little as possible. Some had bad dispositions and would peck your hand viciously even to drawing blood if you attempted to check the nest. Primadonnas would abandon the project if circumstances were not to their liking.

There were rewards, however, for both hens and people when a mother made her debut with a brood of fuzzy little chicks clustered around her. Eleven to thirteen little ones out of a setting of fifteen eggs was considered a good hatch. Why fifteen? Because that was about all the eggs an average size hen could cover.

It was an amusing sight to watch the mother hen's antics and hear her conversation as she managed her brood. She had a distinctive call when she summoned them for a morsel of food, a bug or a fat worm.

There were other calls when a hawk was sighted or a thunder shower came up suddenly that brought her little flock dashing to the shelter of her body and wings as she squatted on the ground, hovering them beneath her until the danger had passed.

A setting hen, before and after her chicks are hatched, has a way all her own. She can be contrary or cooperative. She will flop your legs if she thinks you are going to harm her young. The incubator and the commercial hatchery crowded her out of the setting room in the hen house. Somehow, the barnyard is not the same without her. We even miss the strutting roosters who helped her scratch for special morsels of food.

FORGOTTEN LUXURIES

As country boys, my neighbor and I knew every slippery elm tree for two miles along the Nishnabotna River. With a sharp jackknife we would cut out a small section of bark clear in to the sapwood. On the underside was a layer of soft, spongy, fiberous material that when chewed filled your mouth with a sweetish slippery substance we were sure must be something akin to tobacco.

In early spring there were areas in the prairie meadow that were blood red with wild strawberries, seldom larger than a man's thumbnail, with a delicacy of flavor that kept you searching for more. Neither bumblebees nor prairie rattlers could frighten us away from such a feast for long.

If we were lucky with hooks, lines, and a willow pole in the bayous along the river, there was a string of bullheads to clean for lunch. A handful of wild onions was not always welcome at our house but they, along with a few luscious leaves of sheep sorrel, added a tangy touch to a salad of early lettuce from the garden. A little later in the spring there were sponge mushrooms (morels to some) fried in butter and served with scrambled eggs.

Autumn brought its delicacies to the pockets of hungry boys. There were wads of whitish, astringent gum garnered from the rosin weeds or compass plant; pockets full of red haws or wild plums. There were three kinds, blue, red and freestone yellow. They took a lot of cooking to make them edible. Who could forget the spicy taste of wild grapes still hanging on the vines after the first light frost.

There were wild crabs, not much larger than a wild plum. They were so hard they couldn't be eaten raw. They had to be boiled off a few times and sweetened before they were edible.

A boy or a girl never needed to go hungry along the Middle Border, at least not for long.

THE COUNTRY PREACHER

Country preachers were almost like circuit riders until well into the twentieth century. Every church member was obligated to entertain him and his entire family at least once a year if not more. It was an important occasion at our farmhouse. It meant shaking out the best linen, polishing the silver, selecting the nicest serving dishes, and planning a menu that would have qualified for Thanksgiving. The salaries of country preachers were low, housing was often mediocre, but the food was good.

My mother was a Presbyterian. We had a tall, thin, dark complexioned deep-voiced minister with a wife and four children. We always arranged to entertain them in the summer or early autumn when the children could be out-doors. The Reverend was especially fond of my mother's mince pie. He used to say, "it had a flavor all its own." My mother always lived in fear and trembling lest my father would make good his threat to tell him why. She always flavored her mince meat with a good shot of fruit brandy, blackberry, apricot, or peach.

The country preacher was not only entertained frequently but he was also showered with food from the farmer's caves and pantries. There were hams, sausage, a quarter of beef, home canned products, as well as hay and grain for the horse or team he drove on calls.

Preachers with both town and country charges actually made calls. They not only called on the sick and "shut-ins," but on all the members. If the preacher happened to arrive at meal time, of course he dined with the family on their regular fare. Occasionally he appeared at inconvenient times, but he was always welcome. Even the routine of country churches seems to have changed. Today, ministers who make calls are as scarce as the saddlebags of a circuit rider.

NO SUBSTITUTE FOR KNOWLEDGE

"That person only got through the eighth grade in a country school!" This is sometimes spoken with a touch of amazement, when observing a successful man or woman. The circumstances in those humble surroundings were right for the acquisition of basic knowledge. From primary to the eighth grade, a child moved from class to class, grade to grade in the same room with students at all levels of the educational progress. There was nothing to prevent a youngster from listening in on the recitations of his associates who were doing more advanced work. Furthermore, if there is anything to the subconscious absorption of knowledge the one room country school was an excellent laboratory.

Some of the skills that were taught may no longer be important, but there is no substitute for knowledge. We mastered the alphabet before we learned to read. The champion speller held a post of honor in the student body. The Spencerian technique of handwriting is no longer in style, but it was legible and it was beautiful. That cannot be said of modern penmanship. We learned how to compute the amount of ear corn in a crib, grain in a bin, and hay in a stack. It may be out of style to be able to read, to write, to spell or to figure, but such abilities add to the stature of any human being. They have been found useful by those who left the one-room schools of long ago. For many of them an eighth grade education in a country school was all they needed to open the door to achievement.

The teachers who taught them were often young, but they believed in America and they were dedicated. They taught all things in all grades but they did it well.

COUNTRY TALK

The vernacular and the phraseology of the Middle Border is as unique as it is in various other geographical areas of the United States. Such statements as, "Sometimes things fix themselves better than you can fix them," are often localized in families or neighborhoods. Even so they are passed on from generation to generation. The observation simply means that things often come out all right if you will just let them alone. Things are fouled up with too much meddling about as often as they go wrong without it.

When a thunderstorm moved in, my father used to say, "There goes Uncle Billy's tater-wagon." Where the expression came from I do not know. It may have originated to amuse and to quiet the fears of children.

Expressions often varied widely from one neighborhood to another. In one area, if we plowed, planted, or cultivated a field from corner to corner, we referred to the action as going "cattywampus." Sometimes not more than ten miles away, people referred to the practice as "skygodlin."

I was visiting with a farmer in his barnyard one day when a neighbor who had been helping with the haying drove out of the yard with his team and hayrack. The man he had been helping called after him. "Holler when it hurts, Henry." The statement would have been Greek to a city dweller. Even a nearby neighbor might not have translated the remark. It carried a double meaning, an expression of appreciation and a commitment to return the favor of help whenever it was needed.

"It takes a half a day to start a harrow," is an old expression implying that the simplest task often takes longer to perform than you anticipate.

"Make hay while the sun shines" is an old admonition that is literally true. Certainly you don't want hay to get wet after it has been cut. You need dry weather to cure it for baling or stacking.

"If it rains while the sun shines, it will rain again tomorrow," doesn't always prove true, but often enough to deserve your attention. "Rain before seven (a.m.) quit before eleven" is often true. "A swarm of bees in May is worth a load of hay. A swarm of bees in June is worth a silver spoon. A swarm of bees in July isn't worth a fly," simply means that bees must swarm before mid-summer; otherwise they will not make any more than enough honey to feed themselves through the winter.

You can do without a dictionary in the country, but you can use an interpreter of idiomatic expressions.

HAYSHEDS

Building costs have not always been as high as they are today. Money, however, was scarce. Ten percent interest was not uncommon. Lumber was almost unavailable and expensive. Steel was unknown along the Middle Border. If suitable clay was available, bricks were often burned at or near the site, but they were hardly acceptable for sheds and other livestock shelters.

The hills were covered with prairie grasses. The valleys were full of long, coarse blue stem and prairie grass that grew higher than a man's head on horseback. If laid on a supporting framework it should make an acceptable roof and it did, especially when laid straight up and down the slope of a shed roof. It would last at least a season and sometimes more. In the summer time it would leak a little during a heavy summer rain. The floor would get muddy but, more than ever, it became a cool haven on a hot July day. Especially if the wind was in the right direction to provide a draft.

Countrymen who threshed small grain either out of the shock in midsummer or the stack in early autumn often erected the bare framework of a shed open on one side, sometimes using old woven wire around the sides. It would be located near where the thresher was going to "spot" the separator so the straw could be blown over the frame and stacked on top of it. The technique provided a warm, storm proof shelter that was ideal for livestock. If the interior needed bedding, straw was right around the corner of the shed. Oat straw especially would keep body and soul together for either horses or cattle until a blizzard had blown itself out.

The owner of a hay or straw shed had to be alert to the condition of the roof. Green poles cut from a nearby timber made a strong framework that would support the weight of a straw stack above it for at least a season, sometimes longer. Once the framing began to deteriorate it had to be abandoned. If it collapsed on livestock, animals could be smothered. Such shelters served early settlers well. They were warm and inexpensive.

FLYNETS

The coming of fly time in early summer created problems for us in the days of horse power farming. Horseflies, even the common housefly, could make life miserable for a team and workmen, especially on a hot day. Insecticides were largely unknown.

When the fly problem appeared, we resorted to flynets for the protection of horses. There were three main types, leather nets generally favored for buggy or carriage horses, a heavy fishcord type used on work horses, and a fancy, light weight type of net often used on buggy or carriage horses for special dress-up occasions.

In all cases the nets covered the back and sides of the horse, extending down to the knee and hock joint. The cords or strips of leather were about a half-inch apart, with fabric or leather reinforcements running at right angles to the cords extending in perpendicular lines. The nets had strings or straps that were fastened to the backband, the collar, the hames and the breeching straps when it was placed over the horse's back. Once attached it could be left in place and removed with the harness thus becoming a permanent part of the equipment for the summer.

Hood type nets that covered the horse's head and ears were available, but they were not used extensively except with the fancy cord nets used for dress occasions. The latter net differed a little from the heavy cord and leather types used on driving and work teams. They were more on the order of a fish net with cords arranged in a pattern of one inch squares. They were generally off white in color and had to be laundered occasionally to make a good showing. The leather nets were customarily brown leather, the cord nets for work horses were yellow with black or brown mottling. They were treated with a wax-like substance to make them more resistant to sweat and weather.

Nets were somewhat of a nuisance to handle in connection with harness but they made a horse or a team much more comfortable and easier to handle.

44

GRANDMOTHER'S FLOWER GARDEN

The scarcity of luxury items, long hours of tiring work in the fields and over hot, sheet-iron cookstoves left little time or energy for farmers and their wives to enjoy leisure or enhance the beauty of their surroundings. Even so, the farm woman never lived who did not make some effort to beautify her home, both inside and out.

Farmsteads, even abandoned farm home sites, still show the marks of tender, loving feminine hands. That patch of creamy white and yellow blossoms blooming near that decaying post at the side of the road is butter and eggs. It has long added its splash of color near the decaying wooden gate in front of the house. The towering clump of shrubs that was a heap of color in the spring, just beyond the slanting back porch of the old abandoned house, are the lilacs grandmother planted there when she was a young bride. They were mere tiny sprouts when she brought them from her old home in Ohio.

Those lovely little orchid-like blossoms, only six inches high, spreading like a richly colored purple blanket in a sunny spot along the dooryard fence, are what mother called "flags."

We all adored the dark green clump of foliage along the board sidewalk to the cob house, which became a mass of huge blossoms in late May. "Pineys" we called them. There were white ones, red ones and pink ones. We find them in the seed catalogs under peonies. Scarcely any farm wife's dooryard was without them. They multiplied in any fertile soil if planted in full sun. It was fun to "grabble" small clumps from the parent plant and trade with your neighbor for a color variation you did not have.

There were clumps of "live forever," bleeding hearts, asters, and hollyhocks, the remnant of which still battle with the weeds and tree sprouts for a chance to live and hide the crumbling ruins of an abandoned farm house.

Old fashioned roses, tight petaled pink ones and fluffy yellow ones, fill the corners of abandoned dooryards, blooming profusely, filling the air with their fragrance and recalling memories of a long forgotten era.

46

FRAGRANCE OF YESTERYEAR

It was blue and white, a Chinese jar with a lid that fitted over the opening, but not too tightly. It stood on a shelf in the kitchen just in front of four blue plates and beside a paneled silver syrup pitcher with a hinged top. But the rose jar had the most prominent position. I was allowed to remove the lid only for a few moments so the sweetness of spices and roses that had faded long ago could permeate the room.

The fragrance of its multicolored, crumbling petals recalled the memory of long forgotten joys and sorrows. Into grandmother's rose jar had gone the shattered petals of the rose she wore at her wedding. The few that still held the faint tint of yellow had been gathered from the sunny side of the old-fashioned rose garden she had known as a girl. The fragile remnants of a half-opened bud was from the bouquet of red roses grandfather Joe brought grandmother the day their first child was born. The crimson petals—yes, mother saved them from the sprays on Joe's casket.

There at the very top were the petals of a wild rose, squeezed together in a lump by the sweaty little hand of a small boy long since become an old gray man; a man who still recalls the warm June day he brought them home for his mother.

The fragrance of old, old roses, the aroma of aging spices and memories of long ago sleep within the confines of the ancient rose jar.

Its size, its shape, its color are a vision of yesteryear when things of beauty were rare indeed. Now within its fragrant contents sleep the joys and sorrows that once were real.

FEED SACKS

Who ever heard of making a dress out of feed sacks! There was a healthy trade in such merchandise along the Middle Border during the depression years and the 1940s. Various mills marketed poultry feeds in 100 pound bags of patterned cotton cloth. These were much in demand among farm wives, and even townspeople, for dresses, blouses, housecoats, and various garments.

Sometimes the problem was to obtain a sufficient number of sacks of the same pattern and color for a specific project. This started a brisk market among housewives, both barter and cash. The going price was twenty-five cents each, but they must not have any snags or tears. Many a colorful blouse, skirt, apron, or dress had its origin in an assortment of feed sacks.

The colorful fabrics made up into bright, gay colored shorts, shirts, and jackets to serve as children's summer play clothes. They objected to them for school attire lest they suffer the ridicule of their playmates whose parents might be a bit more affluent.

Not only did feed sacks find their way into clothes closets, but they were pressed into service as decorative features of the home. Many a flowered bag ended its career as a window curtain. Feminine hands often added the decorative touch of a crocheted edge, which along with a pretty pattern provided a colorful cover for a bridge table, a sideboard, or a dresser top.

Frugality was the watchword during the trying times of the 1930s when farm prices sank to their lowest levels in history. Corn reached a low of nine cents a bushel. Some farmers used it for fuel in their heating stoves as it was cheaper than coal. Heavy hogs sold for as little as a cent a pound, stock cows a cent and a half. No one in the country could afford to waste anything, least of all, cloth bags of any kind. Even the white flour sacks made excellent dish towels.

THE HORSETRADER

In the days of dirt roads and only a few automobiles, we could always be sure summer had arrived when we saw the first horsetrader's covered wagon outfit camped on some grassy spot along a country road. A few of the more affluent sported vehicles with a semi-rigid shelter, even to the extent of a door in the rear and a window or two. Sometimes part of a length of stovepipe projected above the roof to provide a vent for a small oil stove inside the wagon; shelter for use when the weather could not permit cooking outside.

There was always a string of horses, trading stock (snides) as his customers called them. The "string" numbered anywhere from two or three to a dozen or more horses, some good, some not so good. Most farmers had to have several work animals as well as a saddle horse and possibly a driving team for use on the buggy, carriage, buck-board, or spring wagon. Generally a farmer had something he wanted to "trade off." Possibly he thought he was shrewd enough to improve the quality of his stable of either draft or light horses.

When dealing with a professional horsetrader, the rule was "caveat emptor," let the buyer beware. You could generally depend on what a trader told you about a horse, but it was what he didn't tell you that often made the difference. It was also wise to watch the conversation. The statement that a woman could handle a horse as good as a man, might mean that no one could control him. One had to be on the lookout for spavins, ringbones, bad wire cuts carefully concealed, and scars from fistulas. The trader was equally cautious in his dealing with a farm based customer. A great many of them were well enough posted in the art to stay even with the trader. The one thing that neither of them could compete with was dope. Either party could doctor up stiffness from an early founder or a lame leg so that the weakness wouldn't show until the dope wore off a few hours later.

The horsetrader, his wagon, his merchandise hobbled or staked out to graze on the grassy bank of a country road, are all gone. The coming of the pavement and automobiles sounded their death knell.

HORSESHOES

There was a time when you could take your horse to the blacksmith in the nearest town and have him shod, but not any more, because only on rare occasions do you find such a place of business and such an artisan in any town.

Getting a horse's hoofs ready to be shod, in other words trimming away ragged edges or surplus length of a hoof, was a necessary part of the project. The iron shoe had to be shaped in the forge to fit the hoof. Care had to be exercised in nailing the shoe on in order not to get into the tender part of the foot and thus have the horse go lame.

Some blacksmiths, or "smithies" as we called them, were better than others at shaping a hoof and attaching a shoe. A horse's stride could be thrown off or he could be caused to interfere (strike one foot against the other) if the shoes were not placed in the correct position on each foot.

Every blacksmith stocked a large assortment of horseshoes in many sizes and weights. The "flats" were a plain, smooth iron shoe with perforations at the proper points for the nails. The "never-slips" had cone shaped metal corks that projected about a half inch below the bottom of the shoe. They were usually put on at the approach of winter to provide horses with a good footing, or grip, on frozen and snow covered ground, even on an icy surface.

If a blacksmith didn't have the correct size shoes for a horse, he could, if he were a good artisan, make a set out of strap iron. The feet of my Shetland, or Iceland pony were so small that the smithy couldn't fit him from his regular stock of shoes. He not only made a pair of flats to be used in the summer but he also made a pair of never-slips, including the corks.

Now the smithies and their shops, with racks of horseshoes, strap iron, wagon tires, hub rings and caps, homemade brick forges and hand-operated bellows are gone. If there is a machinist in town, he wouldn't know where to start to put shoes on a horse. The only hope now is a few traveling smithies, with portable forges and anvils in a panel job, who make the rounds of society stables, or who will come to your farm by appointment.

DIFFERENT TOOLS AND DIFFERENT WAYS

A farm shop such as we knew at the turn of the 20th century would more nearly resemble an antique shop than it would its modern counterpart with electric welders, power grinders, steel vises, and bright metal hand tools.

Farmers with a penchant for wood working and carpenters used wooden planes exclusively. There were all sizes and lengths among those used for the making of moldings, surfacing, rabbeting, etc. Each was equipped with a flat steel blade held in position by a tapered wooden wedge.

In addition to the flat surface planes, there were molding planes for a multitude of styles. They were shorter and generally more narrow, as small as an inch and a half and two inches wide where the surfacing planes were about three inches. The blades of course were correspondingly more narrow to fit the width of the planes. The molding planes were shorter, being about twelve to sixteen inches in length. A board for surfacing or one to be worked up into moldings was held in place on the bench with a wooden vise that resembled more nearly a clamp.

The ingenious farmer with a mechanical bent made a lot of his own tools and gadgets for the farm. A hand made wooden brace was regular equipment in most shops. Those who were affluent enough to own a wood turning lathe operated with a foot pedal were fortunate indeed. Even those who resorted solely to a shop jackknife could work wonders with such a simple tool.

Lemon squeezers, wooden spoons and forks for the housewife's kitchen were marvels of ingenuity; also gate latches, door latches, shucking pegs, pegs for the hall tree, meat hooks for the smoke house, leather strap hinges, bootjacks, door handles, and drawer pulls were products of the long winter days and evenings.

Fortunate indeed was the man who had renovated an old pot-bellied stove, or better yet, who could afford a six dollar tin heater in his otherwise chilly workshop. A bushel basket of corn cobs would take the chill off of most any rural shop so the boss and the hired hand could be reasonably comfortable in their work.

BUCKSAWS AND SAWBUCKS

Only a few people remain who know what a bucksaw looks like or what to do with it if they had one. If you mentioned needing a sawbuck in order to put the bucksaw to proper use—well, confusion would be heaped upon confusion. Many a cord of wood, four by four by eight feet, has been cut by hand with a bucksaw.

A sawbuck was a stout X frame, generally built of two by fours. The lower portion, about three feet long, was reinforced with one by six braces in order to make it stable. A long limb or pole of wood could be laid across the top of the X parallel with the frame. Whatever length of stove wood was desired was allowed to extend beyond the frame work so the operator of the bucksaw could saw if off and move the pole or limb along the sawbuck in preparation for cutting off another stick of wood. It sounds like a hard, slow process of providing fuel. It was just that.

The bucksaw blade usually measured thirty-eight inches. The wood frame with a tension rod at the top for tightening the blade extended upward twenty-one inches at the front and twenty-six inches at the back. It was intended for one man operation but there was room for an operator at each end. Two people made the task a little faster and a little easier. Subsequent metal frames never seemed as popular as those made of wood. They came too late, and of course neither type could stand against the competition of the powered buzz saw. This failed to take all of the drudgery out of wood-sawing, but it turned a long winter's chore into a few hours of hard, fast labor, usually a neighborhood project.

There is an old cliche that if you cut your own wood it will warm you twice. You didn't have to run a bucksaw very long to become aware of the truth of the statement. It would be difficult to find a wood burning stove now in any farm house on the Middle Border, but you do find fireplaces. They take us back to the beginning again, and echo the call for wood. The modern chain saw will fulfill the need. If you are a "do it yourselfer," you will find the old bucksaw and sawbuck much safer equipment.

CROSSCUT SAWS

A "two-man" crosscut saw has been hanging, unused, in our shop for years. Its modern version, the chain saw, has long since replaced it. When a storm took down a large tree or when we were harvesting logs from our timber to be hauled to a sawmill, the crosscut was an indispensable tool.

Crosscuts varied in length from about five to seven or eight feet, depending upon what you needed to get through the trunk of a large tree or a log, once the tree had been felled. They were of an excellent quality of steel in order to maintain a sharp cutting edge for the teeth.

A crosscut required two men to operate it. A straight, wood handle about an inch and a quarter in diameter was attached to each end. The saw was placed across the log or tree trunk at right angles. The man on one end pulled the saw toward himself. His partner on the other end pulled it back, and so the motion continued until the saw had cut its way through. Once the cut had been opened up and the long blade had sawed its way in to a depth of eight to ten inches, the workmen began driving iron or wooden wedges into the cut to prevent the saw from binding or "pinching."

Once a tree had been felled the trunk could be blocked up to where the workmen could stand up to operate the saw. In the case of felling a tree men of necessity had to be on their knees in order to make the cut as close to the ground as possible. It was tiring work. Since it was usually performed in the winter, the action was sufficient to keep the workmen warm even though they were often wet from their knees down if there was snow on the ground.

Now since the invention of the chain saw, the crosscut is an antique. In fact it is even being used as a decorative object on recreation room walls where it no longer puts a blister on anyone's hand.

CORN GRINDING

The first corn grinder in our neighborhood was a horse power machine. It was shaped like an hour glass. It stood about five feet high. The upper half or the hopper held five or six bushels of corn. A pole with a single-tree at the one end was attached to the mechanism that turned the burrs. A horse was hitched to the single-tree and was driven in a circle around the grinder. When a hopper full had been ground the horse was stopped, a wagon brought in and the ground corn that had fallen into the bottom half of the grinder was scooped up. The hopper was then refilled with whole grain or ear corn and the process repeated. It was slow and tedious work but the owners were convinced it was profitable.

The old horsepower grinders proved the value of ground feed for livestock and poultry. They were the forerunner of power driven grinders, hammermills and rollers. Their source of power has gone from horses to gasoline engines, power take-offs on tractors, and electric motors.

In the day of the horse grinder, fifty to seventy-five bushels of grain was a day's work for two men. Now it is a forty-five minute job with a portable grinder and two men. There were no augers and no elevators. All grain had to be moved with a scoop shovel and manpower. There were few tasks as suffocating as scooping corn out of a crib or a bin on a hot summer day to be ground.

Only a few early-day farm operators believed in crushing or grinding whole grain as a ration for livestock of any type. They were the innovators who charted a course for what has became almost a universal practice.

HARROWS AND HARROW CARTS

We used to have a saying in our house that sometimes it takes half a day to start a harrow. It simply meant that occasionally it requires much more time to perform some simple task than we anticipate.

There was nothing complicated about hitching three or four horses to a harrow and have them drag you and the implement over plowed ground in a cloud of dust. It did prepare you completely for a good square meal at noon, and again at night and for bed after supper. You were so plastered with dust that a bath was imperative, especially if you were responsible to a mother or a wife. If you didn't have a bathroom you used a washtub.

If you were ingenious and possessed some mechanical ability, there was a labor saving device that didn't cut down the dirt but it certainly made a day behind a harrow much less exhausting. A couple of light weight, iron wheels on a frame about three feet wide with a seat, usually of cast iron, was sometimes hitched on behind the harrow so the driver could ride. The first ones were homemade. They were a real comfort, especially if you had blisters on your feet from walking behind an energetic team of three or four horses.

A cart had advantages and some hazards, especially when it came to turning around at the end of the field. Sometimes things went wrong turning a square corner. If a horse got astraddle the lead chain or stepped on the harrow there was trouble. Even with a trailing cart, the harrowing couldn't be classified as leisure. The driver had to be ingenious at laying out lands, handling his equipment, and taking care of himself if a crisis developed.

64

FEATHERS, FOOD AND FINANCE

There was a time when every farm had its flock of chickens that supplied both eggs and meat as well as some monetary returns. They were the special prerogative of the farm wife, along with the butter she made and the sweet cream she sold.

Raising a flock of young chickens with either setting hens or an incubator involved hours of time, care, and work. Even raising a flock of started chicks purchased at a commercial hatchery is no easy task. There was water to be carried, feeders to be filled, brooder houses to be cleaned, again and again. A thunder shower would always send the housewife dashing to the rescue of young chicks that could drown if they were not rushed into shelter. The doors to coups and other shelters had to be closed every night to prevent losses from varmints. The lady of the house earned every dollar she got from her poultry project. In addition to some cash income there was always a supply of fresh eggs, young frys or baking chickens for the farm table. Such foods were always available on short notice. The profit margin was small but the availability of the product was a comforting thought.

Every grower had her favorite breed of chickens and reasons for her preference. A few of the more popular types were Barred Rocks, Buff Orpingtons, considered excellent for baking and roasting because they were larger and heavier than some other types. The smaller White Leghorns were selected because they were unusually prolific layers.

Their eggs were white but a little smaller than those of birds of other breeds. Our household preferred White Rocks because they combined the features of the heavy breeds along with being reasonably good layers. There were many other breeds of chickens but the above were the most prevalent along the Middle Border.

Home cured bacon and eggs were on the breakfast menu of almost every farm house. Methods of preparing chicken for the table were as varied and numerous as the number of breeds. An early hatch of chicks meant an early spring delicacy of fried chicken, the first of the season. They were large enough at two pounds to be dressed and fried in halves.

The menus included roast chicken, pressed chicken, chicken and noodles, creamed chicken, chicken and dumplings, and cold sliced chicken for supper. The aroma of a corn-fed, farm-raised chicken being fried to a golden brown in a black iron skillet, or roasting in the oven, is an unforgettable memory.

Housewives who are accustomed to buying a chicken packaged in cellophane and spread on a styrofoam platter should have seen farm women dress a chicken, young, old, large or small, in the old days. After being killed they were dipped into a bucket of scalding water to loosen the feathers which could then be removed easily without damage to the skin. Cleaning and cutting up a carcass with a sharp knife required only a few minutes, and the bird was ready for the skillet.

WORK, FOR THE NIGHT IS COMING

It wasn't easy but there wasn't any other way to do it. The ground had to be plowed. It was done with a walking plow and a husky team (or in tough sod, three horses) which turned the grass upside down. Then the ground was disked. Disks came with a seat but they were not the most comfortable things to ride. Walking over freshly plowed and disked ground following a harrow all day, with the wind in your back or your face and the dust rolling up in a cloud, put you in shape for a good night's sleep. There were seats on the corn planters; two of them, one for the man who drove the team and one for his assistant who rode with him and operated the lever back and forth to drop the corn in the row.

Few remember the back breaking labor of following and steering a New Departure walking cultivator from daybreak until sundown, if you wanted to cultivate ten acres of corn a day. You had to know how to manage your implement when turning around at the end of the row or it would collapse in a heap. You would come out of the tangle with a couple of skinned shins. There were no regrets about swapping the New Departure for a Jenny Lind. It didn't have a seat on it, but at least it would stand on its own two wheels. Real progress came rolling in with the high wheeled Badger that had a wooden lever to steer the gangs, and glory be, a seat for the driver.

When corn was laid by, meaning three cultivations before the 4th of July, we started walking between the rows with corn knives or heavy hoes to cut all of the cockleburs and sunflowers.

When people from the cities used to visit us and see long cribs of corn, it was hard for them to believe that every single ear had to be torn from the stalk by hand. Not only did each ear have to be harvested, but it all had to be scooped into the crib by hand. A good corn shucker could bring in eighty to one hundred bushels per day or about eight to ten thousand ears of open-pollinated corn.

Farming wasn't easy, but it was a good life, even at the beginning of the Middle Border with all of its hardships for both men and women.

LETS HAVE OUR PICTURE TAKEN

Photographs of any kind, even after the advent of the wet-plate camera, were rare along the Middle Border. Sometimes an itinerant photographer with a miniature studio and dark room on wheels showed up in a town or community. Occasionally he opened up for business in a vacant building. Getting the family together for the trip to town to have their picture taken was an exciting event.

The background for a photograph was very important. Even the traveling photographer had a few "props," a fancy chair, a book or two for the subject to hold, and usually a crude mountain or ocean view as backdrop. Occasionally he could produce a forest vista or a city street scene.

I have often wondered why the man of the house was always seated in that ornamental chair and his lady standing beside or behind him. It always seemed like it should be the other way around, but the positions were seldom changed.

Those rather stilted but remarkably clear, sharp photos made with wet plates are the only record we have of the people who settled the Middle Border. Very few could afford the services of a portrait or silhouette artist, so they waited for the "picture man" to come around.

Tintypes, taken directly on sensitized tin, were the other available variation of photography. They were popular but small in size and inclined to darken with age. Tintype photographers were among the attractions at County Fairs and July 4th celebrations where they did a land office business out in the open. The sweetheart who came home from such an event without a tintype of herself or her lover just hadn't been to the fair.

Wet-plate cameras were expensive. There were no centers for developing and making of prints. An individual who could afford to invest in the hobby had to have his or her own dark room and all the necessary equipment and chemicals to produce finished pictures. Not many could afford the luxury of either the money or the time required.

The old traveling photographers, with their wet plates and tintypes, and a few silhouette artists served a real need and added to the documentary history of our country until the coming of roll film with cameras that ordinary country folk could afford. With all of our modern equipment, the wet-plate photographs of the William H. Jackson period have never been surpassed.

A few photographers followed the army or western explorers but most of them stayed close to the main lines of travel for the sake of portrait work. Very few ventured out into the by-roads to record the everyday life of country people.

SOAPSTONES

The word soapstone always conjures up in my mind a sensation of cold weather, the sound of sleighbells and snow creaking beneath the steel tires of wagon wheels. The soapstones, eight inches wide by twelve or fourteen inches long and an inch thick, were about the right size to fit in the bottom of the buggy. They were often kept on the back of the cook stove or in the oven in cold weather so they would be ready for use on short notice. They were heavy, weighing about ten pounds, and could not be handled when sufficiently hot to hold heat for any length of time. Therefore a heavy square-cornered or round bail made of a quarter inch rod was attached to one end as a carrying device.

A soapstone or heated bricks placed in the bottom of the buggy or springwagon under your feet kept them warm during a ride that often lasted an hour or more. Even with the aid of such primitive comfort, there was need for ample clothing and lap robes to keep out the cold on a ride to town in an open springwagon with the temperature down to zero and below.

If the rural family didn't boast of owning a soapstone, common clay bricks would serve the purpose. They too could be heated in the oven or on top of the cookstove. When wrapped in a gunny sack they would retain some warmth for several hours. Soapstones and hot bricks have saved many a pioneer foot from freezing on a long winter drive in an open, horse drawn vehicle.

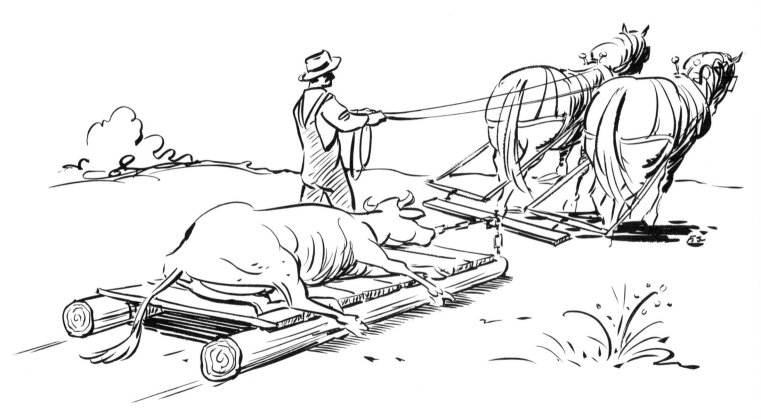

STONEBOATS

A stoneboat was an inexpensive but useful piece of equipment, available to any ingenious countryman. Two straight poles with a diameter of about six inches made suitable runners. They could be about any length desired, but they were usually twelve to sixteen feet, enough length to accommodate all the weight a good team of horses could pull on dry ground. A stoneboat, however, was all season equipment. The skids were floored with two inch planks, if available, to any width desired, usually about five feet. Mortising a spreader pole between the two skids at the front end kept them in line and separated when being pulled. The ideal hitch was a clevis attached to the front end of each pole with a chain through the two of them. A lead chain was then attached to the cross chain and extended to the doubletrees.

A stoneboat had many uses. It was convenient for loading baled hay as you didn't have to lift the bales very high. In winter a good team of horses could pull a sizeable load if the ground was snow covered. In the summer, or at any time on dry ground, the load had to be lighter. The stoneboat was ideal for bringing a crippled or sick animal to the barns. A horse, cow, or steer could be rolled up on it when there would have been no possibility of loading it into the wagon or truck.

The stoneboat really came into its own after the coming of the tractor. With such additional power, two and three-ton loads of baled hay could be hauled from the hay fields even on dry ground.

This primitive equipment was often put to use in moving heavy stationary equipment from place to place on the farm. It could be slid on and off the low floor of the stoneboat with much less effort. It is one of the few ancient devices of early day farming that is still used. In many places it is even superior to the modern lowboy on wheels. It is far less costly and can be assembled in a very short time.

PLOWING STUMP GROUND

Is there anyone still around who has plowed stump ground with a span of mules? It had to be a span of mules if you wanted to live through the ordeal. When mules hit a sudden obstruction they stop. Not so with a team of horses, especially if they have been trained to pull heavy loads until smething gives. Mules were very sensitive to an obstruction. Even a clump of bluestem grass, wild gooseberry bush or a hazelnut sprout would stop them in their tracks.

Plowing with mules saved a lot of broken harness or possibly a plow share. Timber land that had been cleaned by hand a year or more earlier had to be plowed, of course, if you wanted to take a crop off it. A sixteen-inch, wooden beam walking plow, but preferably one with a steel beam, was suitable equipment. The operator walked behind to handle the plow. Well trained mules responded to the commands of "Gee" and "Haw," right and left. The driver tied lines together so they could be adjusted to the proper length around his shoulders, leaving both hands free to steer the plow. Adept as he might be it was impossible to miss all the stumps. Furthermore there was always the possibility that the point of the plow would hit a submerged root. If it did, the implement came to an abrupt stop and so did the mules. If the driver wasn't on guard constantly he could get thrown up on the handles of the plow, especially if the mules took one too many steps. If the plow got caught on a root or a stump it required plenty of brawn, a shower of sweat, and often some well-placed profanity for a man to loosen it by dragging it backwards.

One of the arts of the trade was for the operator to steer the plow as close to every stump as possible. Even without such effort, the task was tiring for both man and mules. All were wringing wet with perspiration on a hot spring or autumn day. When you coupled the day's work and sweat with a few skinned shins, you knew the full meaning of the word exhaustion.

The arrival of the bulldozer and the stump grinder has long since sounded the death knell for the art of plowing stump ground with a walking plow and a span of mules.

WASHING FOR DINNER

Very few early farm houses on the Middle Border knew anything about the luxury of inside plumbing. Housewives worked over benches and dry sinks. The height of luxury was a cistern pump in the kitchen. Eventually oblong or squarish sinks appeared with a drain hole in the bottom beneath which a bucket caught the dishwater. Occasionally an ingenious farmer piped the waste outside to a bottomless barrel sunk in the ground to serve as a makeshift septic tank.

When the season arrived for threshing crews, a bench was placed near the well pump, out in the dooryard. The farm wife provided a couple of wash basins, some bars of soap and towels. Washcloths were a sign of unnecessary affluence. The men "shlushed-off" their faces with a double handful of water.

Such an outside bathroom was a convenience for workmen that they really enjoyed. It was a life saver for the housewife who had no such facilities for a crew of men in her kitchen even though it was often a large room! Furthermore, space was at a premium at threshing time when neighborhood women turned out to help prepare the mountains of food to fill up a crew of hungry field workers.

Baths in the evening had to be taken in a washtub. Sitting down in such a container had its problems. You had to be careful about the amount of water. If you got too much, when your bottom and the tub made contact the surplus water overflowed the tub and flooded the kitchen floor.

One of our ingenious neighbors devised an outdoor summer shower. He mounted a barrel on four stilts and put a canvas around them. The barrel was filled with water in the morning. With the aid of solar heat it would be pleasantly warm by evening. A short piece of hose with a spray head served as a siphon. The bather had to undress and dress in the open or streak to and from the house. Otherwise the improvised shower was a boon to tired perspiring bodies.

GRAIN BINS

Wood lined grain bins in the barns and individual wooden granaries were the only grain storage available to settlers of the Middle Border. Steel bins were not even in the planning stage. Neither was corrugated steel roofing that we used later on to line old wooden bins and frame structures to keep out the rats and mice.

Prior to steel bins the "varmints" were a problem. The only available poison was strychnine. It was dangerous to use because there was no limit to its lethal qualities. Unlike our modern poisons geared specifically to rats and mice, strychnine would kill people or any living mammal. The use of the product was strictly forbidden on our farm.

We trapped and shot rats and constantly exerted every effort to keep them out of buildings, especially grain storage areas. If a rat hole appeared in a wall or the floor we immediately closed it with a piece of tin. If it was a small hole, a pocket tobacco can or the tin top of a snuff box was an ideal tramway blocker. If the holes were too large to be covered with such items, an old automobile license plate was ideal for the purpose.

Thousands of tobacco cans, snuff box lids, and auto license plates, some of them now collectors' items, are nailed over rat holes in wooden bins all up and down the Middle Border. They served a very practical purpose and now are waiting to be rescued by lovers of the old, the artistic and the curious. They may have other values now, but they served a useful purpose for many years and prevented the destruction of quantities of grain. Like most farm people, we tried to prevent as much rodent damage as possible. We were comforted, however, by my father's philosophy, that if we couldn't raise grain any faster than the rats could eat it, we should change our business.

NOXIOUS WEEDS

Early in August was the time we set to walk the cornfield with heavy hoes or corn knives to chop out the cockleburs, sunflowers, pigweed, and butter print, but especially the cockleburs and sunflowers. My father used to say you either had to drive them out of the fields or they would drive you off the farm.

I have often walked a half a mile to get a single cocklebur plant. If it was allowed to go to seed you would have an eight to ten foot square of solid cockleburs the next spring. Nothing but sheep or goats will eat them. They even render the soil somewhat sterile after concentrated growth on an area for two or three years. Since they are annuals, both cockleburs and sunflowers are not difficult to conquer, if you get every single plant.

August along the Middle Border is a hot and unusually dry month. The corn, as they say in the Oklahoma musical, "is as high as an elephant's eye." Cutting weeds between two rows of corn towering above your head with the temperature in the high nineties and no breeze was anything but a cool task. You knew however that the work was productive. Every plant destroyed meant fifty to a hundred less to cut next season.

We always heaved a sigh of relief when we finished walking the last field, three rows to a trip through the field.

Times have changed. Herbicide sprays are not a complete answer but they have lightened the burden. There may be consequences from their continued use but only time will tell. The trouble with chemicals of any kind is that they often kill some things we don't want to kill.

IT CAN BE FIXED

During times of national emergency, country repairmen and blacksmiths were a key factor in keeping the wheels of agriculture rolling. A majority of them were superb artisans at their trade even to the point of making badly needed miniature parts for a machine.

When the country has been at war, repairs for all type of implements were difficult to obtain. The time lag between ordering and receiving a repair part often extended over a period of days or even weeks. It is a frustrating experience when a machine breaks down with grain standing in the field and no repairs.

In such times, the country blacksmith and the little repair shop owner have stepped into the breach, pulled an obsolete repair part out of the junk pile and made it over to fit.

Sometimes he has taken the broken fragments of a cog wheel or an axle and carefully put them back together. Among my relics of the past is a pumpjack, still operational, that was repaired in such a manner. A thin, narrow steel bank neatly welded around the outer edge of one wheel made sure the broken fragments would stay in place after welding. Thanks to such craftsmanship, the cattle at our farm had water within a few hours after the break-down occurred.

Only a few such artisans remain in the rural areas. Most farmers have their own welders. Although some are a bit clumsy with the torch and welding rod, they managed to get things stuck together. The forge has given way to the welder. The smithy and the shop owner in their leather aprons have surrendered to the farmer artisan.

FENCE MENDING

A rainy day on our farm meant fence mending. There were casual repairs that could be made with a minimum of equipment. My favorite horse was saddled, a hammer tied to one side of the pommel, a pair of wire cutters to the other and a small canvas bag of assorted sizes of staples hung over the horn.

To "ride" the pasture fences on a soft spring morning was an unforgettable experience. It was a thrill to inhale the sweet smell of bluegrass, wet with dew and the fragrance of Dutch clover. You were serenaded by yellow breasted meadowlarks. The harsh rasping call of a pheasant cock flushed from his hiding place gave a sense of peace and contentment that just doesn't exist in the seat of a pickup.

Sometimes one got soaked up a bit with a quick spring shower. One of them could hit you before you could untie your shower-proof jacket, or maybe an oil skin tied at the back of your saddle.

"A stitch in time saves nine" was the theory of a fence rider. Restapling a loose wire on a post could prevent a steer or a cow from crowding its head through the wider than normal space, tearing out the staple in the wire above or below and further widening the gap for possible future escape of livestock. A broken wire had to be spliced. If no short pieces that could be used had been left wrapped around nearby posts, there had to be a return trip to make the repairs. Regular checkups often disclosed a post that had been broken or had rotted off. That required another post, a spade, and a tamp stick.

Fence repair, even though it required post setting and restretching wire, can be a pleasant, in fact a delightful experience, rain or shine, spring or autumn.

CORN CRIBS

A crib full of ear corn is beginning to be a rare sight in corn country. Round steel bins, huge tin cans, are rapidly replacing the frame structures for the storage of grain that is seldom harvested in the ear anymore.

Ear corn cribs varied from ten to twelve feet in width, twelve to fourteen feet in height, and usually were constructed in sixteen foot lengths.

Double cribs meant two lines of cribs built parallel to each other, a ten to twelve-foot alleyway between them and a two-way roof that covered each outside structure and the alley between. Such a roof made it possible to construct roof doors on each side. Corn could be elevated to them and spouted to the cribs below.

The framework of such structures for ear corn was often made with poles set in the ground or cement, tied together at the bottom with two by twelve joists to brace the building and keep the floor off the ground. There had to be additional bracing at a height of about six feet to keep the pressure of the corn from breaking out the sides of the crib. The side-walls were made of one by sixes, spaced one and one-half to two inches apart to provide ventilation for the corn. Some cribs were constructed with cement floors laid directly on the ground, but they had a tendency to draw moisture.

Frequently cribs were constructed in a straight line. A few of these were roofed both ways but usually only one way, especially before the coming of elevators when the corn had to be scooped from the shucker's wagon into the crib. Some went unroofed and the grain kept reasonably well until the spring rains set in, when it had to be moved or the owner suffered severe losses from spoiled corn.

Single-line cribs have almost completely disappeared. Some of the doubles have been lined to hold shell corn or revamped for other purposes. Once the revamping process begins, either for grain bins, machinery shelter, hay storage, or some other purpose, they soon lose their original identity. If any remain standing in a few more years, the next generation will inquire, "What's the big shed with wide cracks between the boards on the sides? Why didn't they board them up solid?"

NATIVE LUMBER

Farm buildings of all types, houses, barns, sheds, corn cribs, and even fences were often constructed of what was known in the Mid-West as native lumber. The term was a Mother Hubbard for various varieties of woods.

Cottonwood, elm, and soft maple were more prevalent than hardwoods such as oak, walnut, and hickory. Sawmills moved from place to place wherever there was a good supply of timber, either soft or hard. The mills powered by steam engines could handle logs that were three to four feet in diameter. They charged by the thousand board feet based on whether they had to take the timber off the stump. The price was lower if the owner delivered the logs to the mill. On our farm we chose the latter course. The mill men ricked the green lumber as they sawed it. It was our job to haul it to the farmstead and slat it as we re-ricked it. Without the slats the boards would soon mold and start to rot.

Once the slatted rick was completed we would pile some weight on top to keep it from warping, especially the soft wood. Once it was nailed into place as studding, joists, rafters, etc., it would remain in place and as my father often expressed it, "get harder than the hinges of hell."

Thousands of feet of walnut, oak, and hickory were sawed and used in farm buildings. I have found huge timbers, twelve by twelves used as floor joists in early day houses and barns, some sawed, some adzed, or hewn out by hand. Some of our farm buildings are framed entirely with native lumber. They have stood straight and square for three-quarters of a century.

THE BEST HORSE WON

A cloud of dust far down a dirt road in the back country could mean an approaching vehicle, a drove of cattle being driven to the loading point on the railroad, or it could mean a horse race.

Every little town had its local race horse fans, along with other associates in the sport of kings. There was always someone of the group who owned a horse he thought could run.

There was also an occasional itinerant sportsman who spent the summer months traveling from town to town, usually riding one horse and leading another, looking for a chance to have a little race and make a few bets.

If the traveler succeeded in making a deal with local sportsmen, a place would be selected on some little-used dirt road, a responsible stake holder would be named and the bets put up. A race was seldom set up for less than $100. If the traveling sportsman had a winning horse he could spend a profitable summer. The course usually did not exceed 300 yards. The money involved moved from owner to owners, or vice-versa, in short order.

Two fast horses could cover 900 feet in a few seconds, so the fun was over in a hurry.

Horse racing on a public road has long been a thing of the past. State laws have forbidden practicing the sport of kings in that manner.

SEWING MACHINES

The coming of the sewing machine was a great boon to the women of the Middle Border. At long last they could give their thimbles a rest. In the beginning the flax and cotton had to be spun. Once the thread was ready there was the threading of the loom in preparation for weaving the cloth. When that was finished, there was the pattern to be cut out, the threading of the needle, and the hand sewing of work clothes or dresses. My sightless great grandmother performed all of these tasks within the walls of a one room log cabin in a wooded spot along the western border of Iowa when the state was still young. She was not alone in her labors. There were hundreds of others performing the same tasks.

The coming of the sewing machine was like a new lease on life. The time-consuming task of hand stitching had ended. The early machines had a wide pedal at the bottom of the framework which the lady operated with her feet, leaving both hands free to guide what she was sewing underneath the needle that worked with amazing rapidity, depending upon how rapidly she peddled. With the arrival of electricity came the electric sewing machine that eliminated the need for the undercarriage and the pedal.

Not everyone could afford one of the early machines. Every newly established household's ambition was, however, to own one.

A breakdown of the sewing machine, especially at a critical time while a wedding or graduation dress was in production, added up to a total family disaster. There was no jumping into the car and running to the nearby sales agency for repairs. They had to be ordered by mail or someone had to be selected to take the train to the nearest city with a service center for repairs.

Sewing machines are still with us, but the table top electrics with all of their gadgets are a far cry from the early foot pedal equipment that brought so much joy and relief to our grandmothers.

FLIES AND A FLY TRAP

The pioneers of the Middle Border were beset with many troublesome problems, not the least of which were insects, especially houseflies.

The onslaught of mosquitos during warm, damp summer weather was enough to "make a Spartan sob." Huge green-headed horseflies could come close to driving a team of horses into a frenzy, especially on a hot day when they had been sweating under the strain of pulling a moving machine or a cultivator.

The ever present problem for farm families, from early spring until after a killing frost, was the housefly. He and his kind were everywhere, in the house, around the swill barrel, in the stable, the cow shed and the feed yard.

Shelling, threshing, and haying crews were often served their noon meal on an improvised table in a shady spot on the lawn. There was the eternal problem of houseflies. Of course they were just as bad in the house as they were out-doors.

Screenwire was unknown at the time. The housewife and the neighborhood women who helped each other with the meal would cut leafy branches off the trees and take turns waving them over the tables to keep the flies from getting stuck or drowned in the food. Sometimes the older children were enlisted to relieve the ladies.

Eventually someone came up with sticky flypaper and screen wire traps. How much they reduced the fly population is questionable but they certainly caught a lot of flies. The traps were round, made of screen wire with a tin lid at the top. The bottom was a cone shaped device that extended up into the interior with a small opening about half an inch in diameter at the peak of the cone.

The trap had legs that elevated it about three inches above the floor or table top. A pie tin or shallow pan containing sweetened water or thin syrup was placed directly beneath the cone. Flies would gather there to feast. When satisfied or frightened they would fly straight up through the opening in the cone and find themselves trapped. It never seemed to occur to them to get out the same way they got in.

The traps came in various sizes from table models about six inches in diameter and twelve to sixteen inches in height to large models, some twelve inches in diameter and as much as twenty-four to thirty inches high that stood on the floor.

The coming of window screens and screen doors was a blessing to both men and women. Even after their introduction there was still need for sticky flypaper to hold down the fly population in the house. Several thicknesses of newspaper, shredded along the edge and tacked to the top of the entrance doors helped. Such methods are old fashioned but they still work.

FEATHER BEDS

If you have never slept on a feather bed, much less in one and under another on a cold winter night in an unheated bedroom, you have never experienced real comfort. There is a softness about the support they give your body and the way they fluff up around you that must be something akin to sleeping on a cloud. The feather comforter you slept under in the winter was a little thinner than the feather tick you slept on

If the comforter wasn't available then a feather tick would do. It could be down below freezing in the bedroom and you would never know it. That is, you wouldn't be aware of the temperature until it came time to crawl out of your fantastically soft, warm nest of feathers.

The feathers for a feather tick had to be carefully selected for maximum comfort. Wing and tail feathers were unacceptable. The quills were coarse enough so they would poke through the ticking and jab the occupant. The finer the feathers, usually from geese and ducks, the more delightful the night's rest. Sometimes the down from the fowls would be added to the tick or mattress, but it was usually reserved for the pillows.

The most dramatic descriptions of the so-called restful mattresses can't begin to inspire the admiration of anyone who has spent a night in the luxurious comfort of a feather bed. They may not have been sanitary but they spelled comfort.

A feather bed was one of the first things to go into a west-bound covered wagon and one of the last to be discarded if it ever came to that. No bride's hope chest was complete without a feather bed, a feather comforter and down-filled pillows. Such equipment made life bearable even when placed on springless beds supported by wooden slats. A household with an ample supply of featherbeds, feather comforters and pillows was indeed affluent.

97

FOOD WAS CHEAP

Yes, we bought beef steak for ten cents a pound. It didn't come on a styrofoam platter wrapped in cellophane. The butcher opened the door to his walk-in cooler, lifted a hind or a front quarter of a beef carcass off the hook, laid it on the square or round, wood butcher's block and sliced off what you wanted, loin, round, chuck, or rump roast. He tossed it on his spring scales, wrapped it in brown butcher's paper and it was yours.

We could buy ten pounds of granulated sugar for a dollar. The grocer scooped it out of a barrel and sacked it in a heavy paper bag. If you ordered coffee, the whole beans came in cloth bags. It was scooped out and poured into the huge hand-powered grinder that stood on the counter. The aroma that permeated the air while those beans were being ground was delightful. Navy beans, like coffee, came in cloth bags and were measured out to the buyer. Soda crackers arrived in barrels, dried fruits in wooden boxes, vinegar was measured out of the barrel into your own jug, as was molasses and coal oil for your lamps. The earliest bakery cookies were shipped in tin display boxes with a glass like window in front so you could see the different varieties.

You made your selection, the grocer sacked your order and accepted your count.

The earliest "shipped in" bakery bread was unwrapped. It arrived in large boxes about two by three feet and two feet high. They had wooden bottoms and hinged wooden lids with enough framing to support canvas sidewalls. Efficient housewives looked upon "shipped in" bread with a jaundiced eye. They did this not because of any such nonsense as sanitation, but because many of them adhered to the view that only lazy women bought bread.

About the only things that came packaged were the limited assortment of canned goods. These were a few fruits and vegetables and cove oysters. Even people who bought "canned goods" were looked upon as lazy, extravagant, or just plain wealthy.

Yes, food and paper bags were cheap but there were no added material and labor costs in the form of individual packaging to add to our problem of pollution and trash disposal. The flood of jars, cartons, cellophane bags, plastic bottles and jugs, styrofoam platters and containers was still unborn. We bought our food in the bulk. That is, what we didn't grow and process ourselves.

COOKSTOVES

The life of a farm family on the Middle Border centered around a commodious kitchen, and the focus of the kitchen itself was on the cookstove. Sometimes this was a plain cast iron unit, but occasionally it was trimmed with the housewife's favorite color of enamel. Generally at one end stood a cob box or some suitable container for fuel. Cobs or finely split kindling were needed to start a quick fire. Some fuel boxes were compartmentalized, one side for tinder, the other for larger sticks of wood.

Hoods over the top of stoves to catch fumes and grease are not new; they were standard equipment on cookstoves. They had a balanced roll down door so food could be placed in them and kept warm. They were also a convenient place in which to keep seasonings where they would be dry and usable at all times. Round openings in the stove top were closed with removable lids. If the housewife wanted to hurry a kettle of potatoes or a skillet of meat she could, with the aid of a detachable metal handle or lifter, remove a lid. Thus the food container was much closer to the open fire. In fact, if the draft was open it would draw the open flame across the stove underneath the opening. This action also warmed the water in the reservoir at the opposite end of the stove from the fuel box. Likewise it circulated the heat around the oven just below the stove top.

The oven of the kitchen range rendered a multitude of services. Many a child returning from country school in the winter would be seated on a chair in front of the stove, and his wet feet placed in the oven to dry. Half-frozen baby pigs and lambs were thawed out and dried in its warm interior, with the aid of a slow fire, of course, and with the oven door left open. It was also the only quick dryer for a blouse, a pair of hose, or socks.

Many a master farm cook who helped to settle the Middle Border never surrendered completely to modern gas and electric cooking. In some little out-building you could find a cookstove. Thin columns of smoke curled upwards from an improvised chimney on certain days of the week. The closer you came to it the more readily you caught the delightful aroma of homemade bread, ginger and sour cream cookies, or a pan of bright yellow cornbread. Of course, why waste the fire? There on the back of the old stove stood a black iron kettle with its simmering contents of ham hocks and beans.

CROCKS AND JARS

Ceramic products, such as crocks, jars, bottles, and various other vessels, often produced locally, were a great convenience for country people. They were inexpensive; some were colorful and served a multitude of purposes.

Gallon size, off white, round crocks were favorites among housewives for storing milk, cream, pressed chicken, pickled pigs feet, all sorts of food items.

Ceramic jars were made with lids that fit into the recessed top edge of the container, after which they could be more firmly attached with a heavy wire clamp that worked on tension. Colors varied but the jars were generally dark or mottled brown.

The gallon crocks sold for ten cents each, sometimes on special at a dollar a dozen. If one suffered a fatal accident, the crying was done over the spilled milk, not the vessel. We even used such crocks to water sows penned up for farrowing. By nailing a board across one corner of the pen, the crock could be placed in the space to prevent the sow from upsetting it. Sometimes a particularly energetic critter would succeed in rooting it out, giving it a toss and breaking it but we always had a supply of replacements on hand.

The potters who produced such useful and inexpensive items also manufactured ceramic churns, drinking water fountains for school rooms, as well as large jars. The latter were round with perpendicular sides. They ranged through sizes of one, three, five, ten, and often twenty gallons. Like their smaller counterparts they ranged in color from off white to dark brown. Like the crocks and jars, they had a multitude of uses. One could find them filled with lard, pickles, beef in the process of being corned, pork being cured, eggs in dry salt or water glass, and sometimes dry products such as cornmeal, dry beans, potatoes, carrots, etc.

The ten cent crocks and ceramic fruit jars are no longer a dollar a dozen; they are sought-after antiques. Originally they were just useful containers, now a collector's pride and joy.

THE POTATO HOLE

Basements were almost unheard of in early country homes, but everyone had a potato hole. In the first place brick for walls was hard to come by, unless the quantity you needed was sufficient to justify burning them nearby or at the site of the building. This of course depended upon the presence of good quality clay. Cement as we know it today was unavailable. Who ever heard of cement blocks? A family considered itself fortunate if sufficient brick could be found and laid up in lime mortar to wall up and crown the roof of a cave for the storage of food and protection from prairie cyclones and storms.

If the proper building materials were not available, then a potato hole was indispensable. Snow and freezing temperatures made the use of it inconvenient during the winter.

A great many families adopted a policy of digging the potato hole under the house and cutting a trap door in the floor, generally the kitchen. The housewife or her children could replenish the supply of potatoes without having to go outside in foul weather. The heat from the stoves in the house above prevented any freezing of the vegetable supply.

Frequently when the old pioneer house is moved or destroyed there is a distinct depression under the old kitchen wing. We do not need to speculate about its possible use. It is without doubt, the remnants of the potato hole. Like the cave it served a dual purpose as a shelter in the event of a storm.

Wooden steps led down to the excavated area where bins were provided for the winter storage of potatoes, barrels of apples and other types of vegetables that require a dark, cool place. We can easily visualize ample supplies of sauerkraut, homemade pickles, home-canned fruit, and molasses stacked away in safe keeping for winter use. Early families were largely self-sustaining. With such a well stocked potato hole or cave close by and a cistern pump in the kitchen, a rural family could withstand a long siege of bad weather.

HORSERADISH

It was a hardship to sit down to a dinner of home-cured ham and beans in the country and not be able to improve the meat with a dash of home-grown horseradish. Since it was perennial and required no cultivation there was no real excuse for being without such a delicacy. It would grow in odd corners, fence rows, or any place where it could get plenty of sun. Its long-pointed, light green leaves that grew to a height of twenty to thirty inches made the plant easy to spot. We started digging the off-white roots as soon as the ground thawed and the leaves began to start their growth. It was important when we washed the roots to cut off the crown at the top of the root to be reset in the patch where it could continue its growth. Horseradish is a hardy plant, but any patch can be destroyed by continuous digging without resetting the crowns.

The roots, once dug, washed, with the crowns removed, were ready for grinding. Once the process was started, the aroma from the crushing of the roots was so strong it brought a continuous flow of tears to the operator of the grinder.

Anyone who has not tasted home-grown and processed horseradish doesn't know how hot it can be. By comparison, red pepper is a mild product. With all due respect to the commercial variety, it doesn't begin to compare with the real product, fresh out of the ground. Once processed it begins to lose its strength, which is evidence of why the home-grown variety is much superior to the kind you buy in a bottle.

SAUERKRAUT

Nowadays few people ever think of getting sauerkraut out of anything but a can. There was a time when most farm families along the Middle Border never dreamed of starting the winter with less than a barrel of kraut in the cave.

Every farm garden had rows of cabbage that both the farmer and his wife stood guard over in an effort to stand off any invasion of insects. When the heads were mature there followed the process of chopping, salting, and stomping with a wooden stomper until the mixture was solidly packed in the container. The stomping process continued until each layer of cabbage was submerged in its own juice. There were several types of cabbage choppers. Some, for use with large containers, had handles twenty-four inches long with flat blades as large as a light-weight garden hoe. They were man-sized tools.

A favorite of some operators was made of a board eight inches wide and about twenty-six inches long. Two cutting blades were recessed into the bottom at an angle. They could be adjusted to alter the fineness at which the head was to be shredded. Two inch wide strips of wood along each side of the cutting board guided a six by seven inch box-like frame into which a head of cabbage could be placed. When this was pushed back and forth the slanting knives sliced the cabbage to the fineness desired. The entire device could be laid across the top of a round ceramic jar or other container made ready to receive the cabbage.

Some ladies preferred even smaller types that could be held in one hand. Usually there were two blades that crossed in the center, making what appeared to be four cutting surfaces. The entire tool was not over eight inches high with an incorporated hand grip that could be grasped easily with one hand. The cabbage was chopped in an ordinary wooden bowl or on a flat wooden surface. It required a lot of chopping to fill a fifty-gallon wooden barrel with shredded cabbage. Local grocery stores were usually able to supply such containers since they purchased vinegar in barrel lots.

Home-made kraut, whether made in barrels, stone jars, or fruit jars, had a flavor all its own, even a distinct aroma. On a cold winter day, few things looked better than a plate loaded with home-cured ham, home-made hominy, and home-made kraut.

THE PREACHER GETS A CAR

It was quite common practice during the early days of the automobile for a dealer to take a horse or a team in on a trade for a car. We had a preacher in our small town who drove a rather nice looking pair of bay geldings on his country calls. No one took particular notice of the fact that he usually made his trips on cool days and never seemed to be in much of a hurry.

His congregation decided that he ought to have a car. It could be a great time saver for him. If he would trade his team and buggy in on the deal as down payment, the congregation would put up the balance.

The Reverend was a frugal man and had earned the reputation of being a sharp trader. Never fearing to be out-done, he approached an automobile dealer who had developed the same reputation. After a great many conferences and trial runs, the trade was finally consummated to the apparent satisfaction of all parties concerned. The Reverend enjoyed his new mode of transportation but the team and buggy acquired by the dealer soon disappeared.

One day at a local auction the auto dealer caught the Reverend in the center of an admiring crowd of his friends. Wishing to humiliate the old gentleman, he said, "Reverend, when I took that team of yours home that you traded in on the car, one of those horses had the heaves so bad I didn't dare move him out of a walk."

"Well I declare," said the Reverend.

Pitching his voice a little higher the dealer put the crucial question: "Reverend, did you know that horse had the heaves when you traded him to me?"

"Why yes! Yes! Harry, I knew he had the heaves."

"Why didn't you tell me?" bellowed the automobile dealer.

The reply was quick but toned down as if speaking confidentially. "Of course I knew that horse had the heaves, Harry, but the man I got him from didn't tell me a thing about it so I thought it was a secret. That's the reason I didn't tell you about it."

GRANDMOTHER'S CLAY PIPE

Who ever heard of a clay pipe? Scarcely a person is now alive whose grandmother dated back to the clay pipe period among women of the Middle Border. These pipes were not more than half the size of the modern briar, made of white clay and very fragile. Most users had several so that a nicely tempered, dry one would always be ready in case a favorite was broken.

My own grandmother and one of my great aunts smoked clay pipes. Members of my family reported that those innocent appearing little white pipes could become so strong that you could hardly stay in the same room with the lady who indulged in one.

Some of the users even grew their own tobacco in their gardens. When it was ready for harvest, they would cut the main stem with the leaves and suspend the plant from the ceiling behind the kitchen stove to cure. It was far stronger than the commercial variety. In fact only a few of the more rugged characters could use it.

The clay pipe was the ladies' meerschaum. The bowl was sometimes ornamented with a rather crude pattern of concave perpendicular lines, probably to minimize the heat from the burning tobacco. Since the bowls were small and the smoke short, heat was not too great a problem.

The clay pipe was far more ornamental than a cigarette, but where would a lady go today to buy such a pipe, much less any tobacco plants to grow in her garden. There is a scant possibility that she might find one in an antique shop or a cabinet filled with displays of old family relics.

THE POOR FARM

Will Carleton's nostalgic poem, "Over the Hill to the Poor House," still strikes a responsive chord in the memory of a few old timers. One hundred and sixty acres of publicly owned property, usually located as near the center of the county as possible, was administered by the Board of Supervisors. The land usually had a full complex of farm buildings, in addition to the large dormitory-like residence. It was maintained and kept in order by a man and his wife with such help from the recipients of the county's generosity as they were physically able to give.

Men and women were admitted upon their statement that they were destitute and had no means of support. It was always a last resort, as it was socially degrading.

The family in charge operated the county farm on a rental basis, usually crop share. In addition they were compensated for the food, laundry, and other personal services provided for the occupants.

The "poor farm" came as close to being self-sustaining as it was possible for the managers to make it. Spring saw the planting of an extensive vegetable garden and an ample supply of potatoes. There was a flock of chickens to supply the table with meat and eggs. The dairy project was not extensive but sufficient to provide milk, cream, and butter.

During the winter months there was fresh pork and beef from livestock raised on the farm. Always the supplemental food supply depended upon the ambition of the tenant, his wife, and the number of able-bodied people who resided at the poor farm. It differed only in name and public attitude from federal and state programs of today.

Some of the huge old poor farm houses have been purchased or leased by private individuals and operated as rest or retirement homes. The farms have been sold and their reason for being long since forgotten.

SNOWSTORMS

A blizzard was almost as frightening to men and women of the Middle Border as the prairie fires that sometimes swept across the country more rapidly than a horse could run. It is difficult to comprehend the problems created by such acts of God when electricity was unknown and powerful tractors, bulldozers and draglines had not even been put on the drawing boards. Routine work and crisis situations had to be performed or mastered by hand or met with horsepower. Jackscrews, levers, pulleys, and human hands had to do what we now do with hydraulic lifts, cranes, front end loaders, and a multitude of other mechanical devices. The devastations of a cyclone or windstorm meant hours of hard tedious hand labor.

A blizzard with piles of drifted snow six to ten feet high would immobilize an entire area of the Middle Border. The immediate problem was to get gates scooped out by hand so teams with wagon loads of hay and feed could get to livestock in isolated lots or pastures. Water tanks had to have the snow scooped out of them. Hog troughs and even hoghouse doors had to be uncovered.

The larders and caves of farm families were well enough stocked with staple foods so that people could last out an almost indefinite siege without resorting to the resources of the nearest town while the work went forward to clear the roads.

However, the expected birth of a baby, the need for a doctor or medicine, or a death during a blizzard required the combined efforts of a neighborhood. Bobsled loads of fifteen or twenty men with scoop shovels would descend on a cut through a hill, or any area drifted shut, and begin an around-the-clock process of opening up the road. Volunteer crews would exchange places while ladies from the area would serve hot coffee and warm food.

Now huge, power driven snowplows, maintainers and bulldozers seldom allow the highways to be closed and then only for brief periods during the worst storms. We have saved the work and lost the fellowship. Now even the rural residents of the Middle Border can live from hand to mouth out of the supermarket with little fear of being isolated by snow.

117

WOODSHEDS

It is doubtful if any farm house along the Middle Border was ever without a woodshed, or some semblance of shelter for fuel. Before the coming of the railroads there was no available coal. Wood frequently had to be hauled a long distance. Once sawed the surplus could be piled or ricked outside. However, a wood house or shed was a great convenience to the housewife. Cobs, kindling, cookstove and heating stove wood for immediate needs were best kept dry.

There were separate bins for cobs and for the two types of firewood. Fuel for the heating stove could be larger, depending upon the size of the fire box. Some heating stoves of cast iron were long and low, generally about thirty inches high by some twenty-six inches wide. They would take a couple of sticks eight to ten inches in diameter and as much as twenty-four inches long. The upright type would not of course accommodate such long chunks.

Fire boxes on the cookstoves varied considerably in size with the capacity of the stove. Cookstove wood was generally cut in twelve to fourteen inch lengths. It could be two or three inches in diameter. Larger chunks had to be split. Split wood was desirable because when dry it made a quick fire, more so than round wood. Rarely was kindling made from boards because lumber was too scarce. Corn cobs were the most available and acceptable kindling. They were a natural harbor for mice, so the housewife never liked the supply in the kitchen to be too plentiful. Replenishing the cob basket daily from the woodshed was a regular chore for one of the children in the family.

We are told that smoke pollutes the atmosphere. This cannot be disputed, but who can forget the delightfully tangy aroma of the smoke from a hardwood fire in a cookstove or fireplace?

119

HIGHWAY MARKINGS

The coming of the automobile to country people in the early 1900s created within them a desire to travel that they had never dared to entertain before. Hard surfaced roads were unknown, but drivers and their families risked the threat of mud to explore new scenes at a minimum of expense.

One of the hazards of traveling by automobile in the first decade of the twentieth century was keeping straight in your directions, driving by the sun or by compass. Roads were not only unsurfaced but unmarked. It was much later that enterprising commercial and auto clubs began to mark roads for the traveler. In many respects their efforts were crude but certainly helpful. One of the early marking systems was the white pole road. A white band was painted around telephone poles at corners to indicate if the driver was to turn or proceed straight ahead. The same procedure was followed through towns and cities. Sometimes the bands had faded or the old poles had been replaced and not yet banded. It was easy to lose one's way.

Publishers eventually issued detailed guide books describing landmarks along the various routes. Directions were often remarkably specific. For example: "After leaving Spartanville, proceed five miles straight west to a four-way corner. You will see a red barn on the right hand side of the road; turn left, proceed north until you see a white windmill tower on the left. Turn right at that point, etc., etc."

There were a number of other marked routes such as the Bluegrass Road marked with a green and white stripe around telephone poles. States often had their own specific markings for interstate travel such as the River to River Road across Iowa designating a route from the Missouri to the Mississippi. The marking was two wavy lines painted on a white background.

Touring in an automobile in the early part of the century required the driver to be pilot, mechanic, and navigator.

ENERGY SHORTAGE—PIONEER STYLE

There were no gas stations when automobiles began their invasion of the Middle West. Likewise there were no garages, no stocks of repairs; in fact, scarcely anyone who knew what to do or how to repair an automobile engine when something went wrong.

Gasoline was of course a constant problem for automobile owners. Some ordered gasoline shipped in by the barrel in order to have a supply at home. A few enterprising tradesmen in the towns followed the same procedure of ordering gasoline in barrels. An automobile owner could purchase small quantities if he could find what we would now call a bulk station. The dispenser was a small, hand-operated pump mounted on a barrel.

By virtue of possessing a few tools, a forge, an anvil, and a certain amount of mechanical "know-how," the small town blacksmith and his shop became the stopping place for automobiles in need of repair. The Smithy was the nearest thing to a mechanic in town.

Livery stable owners began to see the potential of automobile traffic. They were among the first to install gasoline pumps supplied from underground tanks. From that point they progressed to an employee who at least understood the basic principle of an internal combustion engine.

The trail of the automobile through the early days of the Middle Border was long and rugged. Its owner struggled with mud roads, mapped his own cross country trails, searched back streets of small towns for gasoline, and waited for would-be mechanics to learn how to help him repair the motor. The modern motorist has no conception of his pioneer predecessors' problems.

CAN YOU HEAR THE HORN?

Horns have been standard equipment on automobiles from the very beginning. There were one and two cylinder machines in our neighborhood and a Sears and Roebuck high wheeler that had the appearance of a single seated buggy without a tongue or shafts. They all had air horns that operated by squeezing a rubber bulb, generally mounted on the steering column within reach of the driver. The bulb was about the size of a large orange. When depressed it made a deep-throated squawk that sent many a driving horse right up in the air. Getting an automobile around a team and buggy or a single-horse rig on a narrow dirt road required considerable skill on the part of the car owner and the man or lady who was handling the horse.

When the drivers met, the problem was equally as difficult, but could be solved more readily. The owner of the automobile was expected to stop and shut off the motor. Either he or his passenger would get out, walk up to the horse, take the bridle rein and lead the horse past the fearsome vehicle that smelled of gasoline, oil, and probably fresh paint. Quite often the drivers of the horse-drawn vehicles appeared more frightened than the animals.

In due time, one manufacturer developed a warning signal called a Klaxon. Pushing down on a plunger resulted in an ear splitting, rasping sound that could be heard a quarter mile away. Horses that had learned not to fear the old bulbous horns almost went berserk at the sound of a Klaxon.

Now and then some enterprising young blade would install a multiple toned warning signal that operated off the exhaust, on the order of a steam calliope. It was musical and always attracted attention. Somehow these never caught on.

When electric horns came in they spelled the doom of all other signaling devices. It is doubtful if the modern horn clears the road as well as the old bulbous variety, not to mention the Klaxon.

TIN MONEY

Most people called the trade money you received at the grocery store tin money. It came in all denominations of real money, one, five, ten, twenty-five, fifty cents, and a dollar. It wasn't really tin, it was aluminum. When we took butter and eggs to the store and traded them for groceries, the grocer paid out any remaining balance due you in tin money, if you would take it. The tokens had the name of the store embossed on the surface. It wasn't good anywhere except in the store that gave it to you in change. If you accepted such "trade money," the storekeeper was certain you would return to trade it out in his place of business. Some shoppers demanded cash. Grocers would pay in real money if the customer demanded it.

The practice of using such a substitute for currency was supposed to be a trade promotion gimmick on the part of the individual merchant. It is doubtful if it stimulated business very much because the trade territory was limited.

Actually tin money was a forerunner of the profit sharing or trading stamp industry of today. Where the latter is an industry in itself shared by all business people who want to participate, the use of tin money was a project of individual merchants to keep their customers.

There is no longer a market for butter and eggs at the grocery store. The tin money has long since disappeared except as it turns up among the treasures of collectors.

LIVERY STABLES

Before the coming of the automobile a town without a livery stable could scarcely classify itself as a progressive community. The architecture, if you could call it such, was reasonably uniform. There was a center alley high enough to accommodate a team and "rig" (buggy) with the top up. Sometimes there was space enough above for hay storage. In other instances the ceiling of the alley was the roof of the stable. One story, shed-like structures accommodated horse stalls on one side, vehicles and grain bins on the other. A small enclosed area in a corner nearest to the street accommodated the owner's office. Tack of all kinds occupied one corner. Sometimes there was a separate tack room adjoining the office with only a half wall and wire netting above. The latter accommodated single and double harness, a few saddles, extra bridles, bits, girths or cinches, and rawhide buggy whips.

Every livery stable owner who succeeded was proud of his horses and equipment. One of his secrets of success was to have his horses well fed, groomed, and exercised so they would always be ready for a hard drive. An owner always made sure that he had one nice looking team, sufficiently gentle that a lady could handle them. It was important to have his buggies, carriages, road wagons, and in winter time, his sleighs in tip-top condition, painted, clean, axles greased, and ready to go.

Medical doctors often used rental rigs rather than have a problem of caring for a horse or team and buggy. It saved him the expense of a barn, feed and water, providing hay and grain, and harnessing and hitching when an emergency case arose. Some of the better stables would provide a driver, usually a teenage boy.

Traveling men of all varieties with their "grips," newspaper men and all sorts of professional people, visiting relatives who arrived by rail were excellent customers of livery stables. The charges, by the hour or the day, varied as widely as the type of rig desired.

The livery stable was the masculine social center of the town. Many a horse trade, livestock or land deal, was consummated in a haze of tobacco smoke amid the aroma of prairie hay, grain, and leather. This aroma permeated, not only the office but the entire building. In fact it drifted out on the sidewalk and served to attract customers and casual visitors, including ladies who came to rent rigs.

SATURDAY NIGHT IN TOWN

You didn't run to town in a hurry for a loaf of bread or a pound of coffee before the day of automobiles and paved roads. Hitching a team and making a four or five mile drive to the grocery store spoiled half a day, even if the dirt roads were dry. If they were muddy it took an extra half hour or more. Two or three trips to town in a day were inconceivable.

Housewives and their farmer husbands consolidated their shopping lists, generally for a weekly trip to the nearest town. During the winter months it was usually Saturday afternoon, perhaps even all day. Neighbors assembled in the grocery stores, the drug store, meat market, barber shop, or the drygoods store, chatted and exchanged bits of news and, needless to say, some gossip.

Summer months when farm people were in the fields from daylight to dark there was no time for trips to town, except on Saturday night for necessities. These were romantic jaunts for the "small fry" in the family. Even in those days there were oil or gas street lights, huge hanging oil lamps in the stores, all of which added a touch of romance to an evening in town for both the young and old who seldom traveled far beyond the boundaries of their own county.

There were always thrilling moments of conflict on side streets and in shadowy alleys between "town kids" and "country kids." An individual from either group knew better than to travel about in the village alone, day or night. He could wind up with a black eye or loose tooth.

Regardless of hazards, a Saturday night in town was worth the risk.

131

LOCK HIM UP

Small town jails were an indispensable part of every community's social structure. Jails were really small in small towns, often twelve by sixteen or at the most, sixteen by twenty feet. The walls were constructed of two-by-fours laid flat from floor to ceiling and spiked together. They appeared to be a huge block of wood with a roof on it. Two small heavily barred windows furnished some light and ventilation. The cage-like structure was supplied with an ordinary wooden plank door on the inside to keep out the weather. It could be opened or closed by the occupant. The entrance to the structure was supplemented on the outside by a cage-like door of iron bars that the town marshall locked. A cot, a straight back chair, a dipper and bucket of water, a chamber pot and a small stove installed in cold weather, constituted the total equipment. Conveniences were so primitive that an offender was seldom incarcerated for more than a few hours until plans could be made to transport him to the county jail.

Even though security was at a minimum, escapes were uncommon. One prisoner in our local small town jail set fire to one wall with the aid of some waste paper and some matches he had not been relieved of when locked up. The heat and smoke soon forced him to use the contents of his water bucket to extinguish the blaze. These jails were so well built that they are often still standing, usually on private property, having been pressed into service as shops or storage buildings.

Communities that once boasted a full complement of law enforcement services now depend largely upon state patrolmen, county sheriffs and their deputies. Communications are such that they can be reached, more quickly perhaps, than a local town marshall could be located. They are not as colorful as the early day local official who often had his hands full in getting a lawbreaker into the one room jail and in getting his fellow townsmen to serve as deputies. It was imperative, therefore, that he be a fast sprinter and the strongest man in town in order to be sure of making an arrest and then locking up the offender.

SPRINKLER WAGONS

One can scarcely imagine how dusty a dirt road in the country and unpaved town streets can become during extended periods of dry weather. Town and city streets with heavy horse-drawn vehicles and some early automotive traffic could become almost unbearable. Fine powdery dust would accumulate to a depth of several inches. When whipped by even a moderate breeze it would swirl down streets, settling upon shoppers and infiltrating all the stores on main street.

City councils in towns of any size were pushed to develop a solution to the vexing problem. Paving stone of sufficient quality such as cobblestone often had to be shipped great distances at considerable expense. Hard shale bricks that would stand the wear and tear of traffic were almost unknown. There were no machines for laying concrete so any surfacing of that kind had to be ruled out.

There was only one other answer at the time, water to settle the dust. As a result every up and coming town had to have a street sprinkler. Some were commercial types and others were home made affairs put together by enterprising merchants with the help of the local blacksmith. Very few of the early ones operated under pressure. They consisted of a round or oblong tank mounted on the running gear of a wagon. There was an outlet pipe at the rear connected to a pipe running crosswise of the container. Holes were drilled in the bottom of the latter so that when the flow was turned on the water would dribble out the holes. These sprinklers were quite effective and a boon to both town and country people. If used frequently they held the dust in check. When pressurized tanks came in they fanned the water, and thus a tank full would go much farther than it did in the old drip type sprinklers.

The tanks held from five to six hundred gallons of water. Low wheeled running gears were preferred as they allowed the water outlets to be closer to the ground. Sprinklers were drawn, of course, by a team of gentle horses, that even so had to be handled by an adept teamster. Hot dry weather required sprinkling every day. If the dust was allowed to become two or three inches deep, as it could do in a short time with heavy traffic, excessive amounts of water had to be applied to settle it. In any event, sprinklers were life savers for small towns that could not afford paving.

COUNTRY HOTELS

Before the coming of hard surfaced roads and automobiles, the traveling men in the Middle West could readily direct you to the best country hotels in their territory. Like the tramp who knew the warm spots in the gutters, they knew the hosteleries with the best and cleanest beds, the finest food, and the warmest hospitality.

When salesmen traveled by train it wasn't always possible to get home for weekends. No one wanted to spend Sunday in an uncomfortable bed or dine on unsavory food.

Every small town had its hotels, some good, some not so good, and some bad to say the least. Our town had three. One of the hotel runners who met the trains to solicit business used to say, "No matter which one you selected you would wish you had stayed at the other one." Actually that wasn't true. None of them were that undesirable.

One hotel in particular was favorably known for miles around. Traveling men set up their schedules so they could spend Sunday at the Kuntze Hotel. It stood across the railroad tracks from the depot, a five minute walk from where the trains came to a stop. The beds were clean, the front porch was wide and best of all the food was excellent. There was no such thing as a menu. When the dinner bell sounded the family style table was groaning under its load of home cooked delicacies. There were always at least two kinds of meat, chicken and roast beef, baked ham and roast duck, mashed potatoes and American fries, baked beans, coleslaw, garden vegetables in season, home baked bread and country butter, canned fruit for desert, or wedges, not slices, of pie and freshly frosted cake.

The accomodations, the culinary art, the hospitality of some old time country hotels and their family style table could not be surpassed. Today they would be welcomed back with a shout of joy.

THE OPERA HOUSE

"Uncle Tom's Cabin will open at the Opera House at eight o'clock this evening."

From that point the hand bill went into raptures about the traveling cast. Usually it had just returned from a successful tour to Canada, the far west, or some other distinguished whereabouts that no one ever attempted to verify. No one cared, because entertainment, especially in the winter months, was so scarce that the people of the Middle Border welcomed any traveling troupe that came along.

Every town of any consequence had an opera house. These would usually seat at least two or three hundred spectators. The stage, sometimes with a curved front but usually straight, would accommodate a sizeable cast of thespians, musicians, or other entertainers.

The stage curtain was decorated with a forest, ocean side, or city street scene with ads of the local merchants all the way around the edge. Grocers, dry goods owners, barbers, druggists, poolhall operators, butchers, lumber dealers, banks, and elevator owners—all had their space, often in highly ornamented lettering or even incorporated with appropriate vignettes of offices or places of business.

Traveling sign and scene painters were responsible for the art work, some of which had real merit. Not only did they paint the scene on the curtain but also an assortment of moveable wings. Some gave a dimensional effect to forest, seaside or street scenes. Others created a household or shop interior with doors and windows and other decorative effects. There were always two dressing rooms, one for ladies, one for men. Since many of the opera houses were built before plumbing, the two toilets, often referred to as Aunt Jane's, were in the alley at the rear of the building with access through a grade level door.

A town without an opera house just couldn't qualify as socially acceptable. Traveling plays, winter lyceums, musical programs passed them by. A frontier town could do without a lot of things but not without an opera house. The high school senior class play, the music teacher's operetta, even graduation ceremonies, were held in the opera house.

HANDCARTS TO THE RESCUE

No matter how small the midwest town of the early days might be, it had a volunteer fire department, always dominated by the youngest, strongest, most fleet young businessmen in the village.

The equipment was primitive and varied in quantity with the amount of funds available, whether donated or assessed by the city council. The vehicles were two-wheeled hand carts, usually one for a roll of hose and a hand operated suction pump, the other for several extension ladders. In addition to a cross handle there was a knotted rope attached to the front of the carts to provide more space for additional manpower. A good supply of "fire buckets" with bottoms that came to a point, hung from hooks on the carts. They could be used only for carrying water to and pitching it on a fire. If the distraught owner of the burning building had a tank of water near-by, a shallow well or a cistern, one end of the hose could be dropped into it and with the aid of the suction pump, project considerable water to the burning structure. If no such supply was available, the firemen formed a bucket line to the nearest well pump and so fought the blaze the hard way.

The alarm system was a shrill toned bell mounted on a tower outside the fire house. It was operated with a rope. When the summons came the enthusiastic fire fighters burst out of shop doors, professional offices, and banks like frightened sheep, but with an avowed purpose. Often they were hatless and coatless. Their attire ranged from white shirts and aprons to overalls and dress coats. The carts, buckets and all were wheeled out into the street with everyone shouting orders at the top of their voices. Each loyal citizen grabbed a handhold on the knotted rope and started racing for the scene of the fire with amazing speed, stirring up a cloud of dust or splashing through the mud, often spurred on by a pack of yapping dogs. A large clanging bell attached to one of the wheels rang with every revolution spurring the boys on faster and faster.

Motorized equipment has crowded the hand carts into the museums and covered the shirt sleeves, dress coats, and overalls with rubber raincoats and hard hats.

Let us not forget the service of those early patriots who actually had a marked degree of success in quenching fires, saving human lives and property.

THE CHANGING SCENE

Not only the countryside of the Middle Border has changed but the thriving little towns that served the people have changed also. Some have grown into sizable cities. Others have faded away completely, while a few live on, half ghost, half reality. Large or small, alive or starting the long sleep, most of the trappings of the past have disappeared.

When you drive into town, no longer does your glance flash up and down the long lines of pole hitchracks for a place to tie your saddle horse or your team. The hitchracks are gone. Of course you don't need a place to tie, you need a place to park your car. The dusty old main street is paved now. The aroma of hay, grain, and the other fragrances from the livery stable has given way to fumes of gasoline and diesel.

The fire bell, mounted on a slender tower to call the volunteer firemen, has given way to the town's fire whistle with its wailing shriek. It sets every canine howling for miles around.

The fire department's hand powered push carts have been relegated to the nearest museum of historical items. A new, shiny, motorized fire engine has replaced them.

The barber's chair is so modernized you hardly recognize it. The grocery and the drug store have gone self-service. The crowning blow of all is that scarcely a country town is left that sports a soda fountain with a white coated "soda jerk," small round wire-legged tables and wire-backed chairs for the comfort of customers. The huge propeller-like fans, once suspended from the ceiling, have been replaced by an air conditioning unit. The old tin street lights with bulbous heavy glass globes that had to be lighted individually every evening and turned off every morning are usually stored in the attic of the old city hall, unless they have been found and carted away by some avid collector or antique dealer.

The druggist's mortar and pestle sign, the optometrist's eyeglasses, the butcher's steer head, the tobacconist's wooden Indian are all gone, even to the barber's candy stripe barber pole. Some were works of art, some were rather crude, but they helped you find the place you wanted to go. Now with our new efficiency we prowl up and down the street, straining our eyes to read the numbers on a transom window or the name on an entrance door.

There has been a saying in our family for generations that "Things have changed since Willie died." Where Willie was or where or when he died, I do not know, but one thing is for sure, "Things have changed."